The Sherlock Holmes of Saint Louis: Saint Louis Chief of Detectives William Desmond

By

Ken Zimmerman Jr.

The Sherlock Holmes of Saint Louis: Saint Louis Chief of Detectives William Desmond

Copyright 2024 by Ken Zimmerman Jr. Published by Ken Zimmerman Jr. Enterprises www.kenzimmermanjr.com

All rights reserved. You may not reproduce any part of this book, stored in a retrieval system, or transmitted in any form or by any means—electronic, mechanical, photocopy, recording, or any other—except for brief quotations in printed reviews without the prior permission of the publisher.

Published in Saint Louis, Missouri by Ken Zimmerman Jr. Enterprises.

First Edition: April 2024

If you like this book, you can sign up for Ken's newsletter to receive information about future book releases. You can sign up for the newsletter at kenzimmermanjr.com.

Table of Contents

Dedication 7

Introduction 8

Chapter 1 – Detective Billy Desmond 12

Chapter 2 – Established Detective 27

Chapter 3 – 33-Year-Old Chief of Detectives 43

Chapter 4 – Frisco Train Robbery 62

Chapter 5 – Capture of H.H. Holmes 70

Chapter 6 – Second Half of the 1890s 84

Chapter 7 – Ten Years as Chief 96

Chapter 8 – Boodling Case and New Assistant 139

Chapter 9 – 1904 World's Fair 148

Chapter 10 – Tragedy Visits Desmond 158

Chapter 11 – Lord Barrington 164

Chapter 12 – Travesty of Justice 180

Conclusion 187

Other Saint Louis History and True Crime Books 192

Bibliography 193

About the Author 195

Endnote 197

Dedication

I am dedicating this book to Saint Louis Chief of Detectives William Desmond. No Saint Louisan should forget "The Sherlock Holmes of Saint Louis."

Introduction

William Desmond was born on May 10, 1857, to William and Elizabeth Desmond in Massachusetts. While he was still a child, the family moved to Saint Louis. The Desmond family bought 1710 O'Fallon Street, where Chief Desmond lived during his early police career.

Desmond had two sisters, Marie and Eliza. The siblings lived together in the family home at 1710 O'Fallon Street after the death of their parents. On January 9, 1890, Eliza Desmond died after a lengthy illness.[i] Eliza was 37 years old. Born around 1852, Eliza was the oldest of the three siblings. Marie was the youngest as she was born around 1861.

William Desmond joined the

Saint Louis Police Department in either 1876 or 1877.[ii] Desmond must have inflated his age as the board appointed him to the department when Desmond was 19 or 20 years old.

Desmond showed a talent for police work from the beginning of his career. Desmond and his partner Officer Ryan arrested Robert Willis in 1878 for stealing a $7 pair of boots and a fifty-cent smoking pipe from Christian Krueger of 827 Carr Street. The judge sentenced Willis to three months in the Saint Louis Workhouse.[iii]

On July 2, 1881, Desmond arrested Harry Freeman after a foot chase. Freeman, a pick pocket, removed $10 from Annie Roach's purse, while she walked down Franklin Avenue near Sixth Street.[iv]

On October 25, 1881, the Saint Louis Board of Police Commissioners appointed Desmond and Officer Browning to the rank of Detective. Both officers served five years under Captain Huebler in the Third District. The officers stood out amongst their peers for efficiency and diligence in performing their duties.[v]

Officer William Desmond transitioned into his new role of Detective "Billy Desmond." Not long after his appointment, Desmond formed a partnership with Detective Pat Lawlor. Desmond and Lawlor set the standard for detectives during their time together. Both men always said they learned so much from each other that their partnership made them both better detectives.

In his new role, Desmond developed the skills that transformed him into the "Sherlock Holmes of Saint Louis."

Figure 1-Artist Rendering of Chief Desmond Around 1905

Chapter 1 – Detective Billy Desmond

Detective Desmond quickly distinguished himself as a detective. Desmond's peers considered him both tough and dedicated. With his persuasive communication skills combined with his fighting ability, his supervisors often assigned Desmond to tough cases in the "Bloody Third" District.

Desmond preferred talking to people rather than fighting them. Desmond only resorted to restraining suspects when necessary.

Prior to his official appointment, Desmond functioned as a detective with Detective Browning. During one shift, Desmond and Browning stopped Spencer H. Davis and William H. Anderson near

Christy Avenue.

After the detectives arrested the men, they searched Davis and Anderson. The search revealed Davis and Anderson were carrying revolvers, knives, and razors.[vi]

The detectives took both men to the Third District Police Station. The detectives continued questioning Davis and Anderson, which led to a burglary investigation in Bowling Green, Missouri. Bowling Green is a city in Pike County, Missouri about ninety miles north of Saint Louis.

Davis and Anderson disposed of property at the local pawn shops that Detective Desmond linked to the Bowling Green burglary. The victim of the burglary, Mr. J. Dickson, traveled to Saint Louis. Mr. Dickson claimed the property.

Mr. Dickson contacted the Pike

County Sheriff's Office to transport Davis and Anderson back to Pike County for trial.[vii]

In September 1881, the Pike County court sentenced Davis and Anderson to the Missouri State penitentiary. The court sentenced Davis to six years and Anderson to five years in prison.[viii]

Spencer H. Davis entered prison on September 15, 1881. The state released Davis under the three-fourths rule on March 12, 1886.

William H. Anderson entered prison on the same day. The state released Anderson under the three-fourths rule on June 6, 1885.[ix]

In another case on Monday, July 31, 1882, ex-convict Alexander Estes entered the grocery store of John Bilker, 801 Morgan Street. Bilker suffered an epileptic seizure after Estes walked in. Seeing Bilker's helpless state, Estes took $80 in cash, a gold chain and silver watch from the store.[x]

As Bilker recovered from the seizure, he was not aware Estes had taken his valuables. As he regained his senses, he realized someone took his cash and jewelry. Bilker could not remember Estes stealing from him but did see Estes enter the store before he suffered the seizure.[xi] Bilker reported the theft to the Saint Louis Police.

Detective Desmond knew Estes and his hangouts. Desmond caught Estes in a gambling den on Morgan Street between Seventh and Eighth Streets. The gambling den was one block from Bilker's grocery store.[xii]

Based on Desmond's work, the Saint Louis Court sentenced Estes to the Missouri Penitentiary for two years for Grand Larceny on February 24, 1883. Estes entered prison on March 10, 1883.[xiii]

Estes died before he completed his sentence. Pneumonia led to Estes death in the prison hospital on December 6, 1883. Estes died at only twenty-eight years of age.[xiv]

On Monday, February 12, 1883, Detective Desmond and his normal partner, Detective Pat Lawler, were checking on businesses in the Downtown area. Desmond and Lawler entered the City Hotel, at Fourth and Elm Street, where they saw Norman Swartzell playing pool. The detectives arrested Swartzell.[xv]

Swartzell labored on a farm in Ogle County. The farm owner, Thomas McGregor, allowed Swartzell to live on the farm until he suspected the 28-year-old Swartzell of having romantic feelings for McGregor's 13-year-old daughter.[xvi] McGregor fired Swartzell, paid Swartzell his full wages, and kicked him off the farm.

At the end of January 1883, Swartzell invaded the McGregor farmhouse with a loaded revolver. He shot 13-year-old May killing her instantly.[xvii]

80-year-old Thomas McGregor tackled Swartzell, but the younger man freed himself from McGregor's grip. Swartzell shot McGregor in the face. The wound prevented McGregor from speaking.[xviii]

Mrs. McGregor asked Swartzell what he wanted. Swartzell told her he wanted all their money. Mrs. McGregor had not dealt with Swartzell, so she did not know Swartzell. She handed him $60 the couple had to pay their taxes.[xix]

Swartzell fled the farmhouse. If Mr. McGregor died, the Ogle County Sheriff's Office may not have learned Swartzell's identity. Mr. McGregor lived and told the sheriff who attacked the family.[xx]

The Sheriff secured a warrant for Swartzell. Saint Louis Police learned about the warrant after Detectives Desmond and Lawler received a tip about Swartzell staying in Downtown Saint Louis.[xxi]

After the detectives arrested Swartzell, the Ogle County Sheriff picked Swartzell up and placed him in the Ogle County jail. Swartzell avoided the trial and probable death sentence when he died of stomach congestion in early April 1883.[xxii]

On August 6, 1883, Desmond had a narrow escape after arresting a burglar, Robert Harris, at Seventh and Carr Streets. Desmond and Lawler missed finding a firearm when they searched Harris. As they walked along, Harris suddenly tried to draw the concealed weapon.[xxiii]

Desmond saw Harris reach for the gun. Desmond stopped Harris' draw while disarming him. Harris made no further attempts to escape.[xxiv]

Desmond also battled criminals attracted to one of the fastest growing cities in the United States. Pickpockets proved a constant nuisance in a large city like Saint Louis.

Desmond and Lawler arrested a dozen pickpockets during 1883 and charged them with vagrancy. When Desmond and Lawler brought the men before the court, the judge found the pickpockets guilty of vagrancy. The judge gave the convicted men until 6 p.m. to leave town or serve thirty days in jail. The pickpockets caught the first train out of town.

On Christmas night 1884, a group of masked men pulled a brazen robbery on the Cass Avenue Streetcar. Mr. W. Stead rode the streetcar home with six other passengers.

As the streetcar approached Visitation Convent in the 4500 block of Evans Avenue, Mr. Stead heard a gunshot. The streetcar stopped. Two armed men jumped on the rear platform of the streetcar. A single armed robber jumped onto the front of the streetcar.[xxv]

The armed men announced a robbery while threatening the passengers with their guns. Five of the seven passengers ran for the doors. The two shooters at the rear platform let them pass. However, they stopped Mr. Stead and pushed

Stead back to his seat.

One of the robbers pulled Mr. Stead's watch chain and pocket watch from his coat. The forced removal broke the chain. The other robber took the remaining chain from Mr. Stead's pocket.

The robbers took about $4 in cash, coins Mr. Stead tried to hide, and the watch valued at $75.00. They missed $9 in cash in a deep pants pocket.[xxvi]

Mr. H. W. Smith, the other passenger, said he thought the invaders intended to rob the conductor. The robbers clubbed the conductor on the head and threw him into the street after finding his pockets empty. The men turned to robbing the passengers but only took something from Mr. Stead.

Mr. Smith helped the conductor up. The conductor suffered a minor head injury and an injured hand from trying to scuffle with one of the robbers. Saint Louis Police arrived soon after the robbery occurred.[xxvii]

After hearing about the robbery, Detective Desmond thought one of the robbers sounded like Paddy Welsh. Chief of Police Harrigan was furious at the robbery on Christmas Eve Night and sent a squad of detectives to the "Kerry Patch," a tough Irish neighborhood.

Desmond investigated the area near 15th Street and Wash Avenue. The shadows hid Desmond, who saw two men exit 1502 Wash Avenue. Desmond stepped further back into the shadows to watch the men.

Welsh, a recently paroled burglar was the shorter of the two men Desmond watched. Desmond approached Welsh.

Desmond asked what Welsh was

doing to which Welsh swore at Desmond to mind his own business. Desmond saw Welsh go for his pocket. Desmond prevented Welsh from removing Welsh's hand from Welsh's pocket.[xxviii]

Welsh yelled for his accomplice to shoot Desmond, but his partner fled the scene instead. While keeping a grip on Welsh's gun hand, Desmond brought his service revolver down onto Welsh's head staggering Welsh momentarily.

Welsh grabbed Desmond's gun barrel and tried to disarm Desmond. Desmond took Welsh to the ground, freed his revolver, and stood back up. Desmond avoided shooting Welsh by striking Welsh on the head two or three times.

Welsh continued trying to reach his revolver, but Desmond blocked his attempts. After more blows with the revolver, Welsh fell to the ground. Desmond secured Welsh and other officers transported Welsh to the infirmary.[xxix]

Despite repeated strikes to the head, Desmond did not seriously injure Welsh. Welsh still fought with other officers at both the infirmary and the Third District Police Station. Officers booked Welsh for assault and being a felon in possession of a firearm.

Neither Mr. Stead, Mr. Smith nor the conductor could name Welsh as one of the robbers. Mr. Stead and the conductor thought Welsh could be a robber. Since the robbers wore slouch hats and scarves over their faces, the victims could not positively name Welsh.[xxx]

However, Judge Cady fined Welsh $25 for carrying a concealed weapon.[xxxi] $25 is a little over

$750.00 in 2022 money. Judge Cady warned Welsh that Cady would sentence Welsh to jail time in the future.

By 1885, most Saint Louisans, who read the daily newspapers, had heard of Detectives Desmond and Lawler. The crime fighters built a solid reputation with their record of solving crimes.

Figure 2-Artist Rendering of Chief Desmond Questioning a Suspect (Public Domain)

Chapter 2 – Established Detective

On the morning of Wednesday, July 8, 1885, the Coroner's Clerk Jimmy Spaulding rushed into the Police Court at the Four Courts building. Spaulding announced one of the jail inmates waiting in the holding pen had just escaped. While the members of the court sat stunned, Detective Billy Desmond jumped to his feet and rushed out of the courtroom.

The 28-year-old detective ran to the pen just in time to see two legs hanging out of the hole where the other prisoner escaped. Desmond grabbed one of the legs, said "come back here" and forcefully dragged the man back into the pen. Desmond looked down to see notorious St Louis thief Con Foley. When Foley realized Desmond was holding his legs, he surrendered.[xxxii]

Foley quickly named the escaped prisoner as William Clark. Clark was better known by his alias Skippy Dean. Dean had escaped the Saint Louis Jail in an earlier incident during 1881, which led to the murder of Patrick Doran.

Prior to his arrest, Dean was awaiting trial for the robbery of a store on Chouteau Avenue. Witnesses saw Dean running down Eleventh Avenue, where Dean made good his escape.

Authorities eventually caught up with Dean. In Illinois, police arrested Dean for new crimes. By 1887, the Illinois Court sentenced Dean to a long prison sentence in Joliet, Illinois.[xxxiii]

Con Foley continued to bounce in and out of jail. In November

1886, a Saint Louis Court sentenced Foley to 6 months in jail for stealing a $10 overcoat.

Detective Billy Desmond paid particular attention to pawn shops. Desmond continued to check pawn shops after becoming St. Louis Chief of Detectives in 1890.

Desmond attributed his reputation as a "thief taker" to frequenting pawn shops in Downtown St. Louis. Thieves or their fences, stolen property dealers, often sold their ill-gotten gain at the pawn shops.

Running a pawn shop has always been a tough business because shop owners must constantly be on the lookout for people pawning stolen goods in their shops. In the late 19th Century, police detectives worked with pawn shops, as they do today, to try to stop the fencing of goods.

In August 1885, future Saint Louis Chief of Detectives William Desmond and his partner Detective Pat Lawler found a pawn shop purposefully acting as a fence for stolen goods.

On Saturday, August 7, 1885, a citizen named John Mockler was traveling home to 1305 Belt Avenue. During his walk, he stopped to rest at Ninth Street and Washington Avenue. Mockler soon fell asleep.

When Mockler woke up and entered a streetcar, he went into his pocket to check the time. Mockler realized someone had taken his watch, chain, and locket.[xxxiv]

The following Monday, Mr. Mockler reported it to the police. The Chief of Detectives assigned Detectives Desmond and Lawler to the case. They made the rounds of all the pawn shops including Emile Sasse and Son at 806 Franklin Avenue. The proprietors told the detectives they would be on the lookout for the stolen items.

On Thursday, August 13, 1885, Detectives Desmond and Lawler stopped in at Agnew and Reinhold Jewelry Manufacturing Company. The detectives found the watch case, chain, and locket. The only thing missing was the watch itself.

When the detectives asked the jewelers where they obtained the items, they produced a receipt made out to Emile Sasse and Son Pawn Shop. They paid $24.50 for the items considered old gold. The Agnew and Reinhold Jewelry Company used the items to manufacture new jewelry.

The detectives returned to Emile Sasse and Son Pawn Shop. In one of the cases, they found the stolen watch. At first, Emile Sasse, his son Otto and clerk Charlie Woods, who sold the items to Agnew and Reinhold, denied knowing Woods sold stolen property. Eventually they admitted knowing they were fencing stolen property.

The detectives looked through the transaction book and discovered the men were not logging all transactions as required by law. A further check of the inventory turned up other stolen items. Desmond and Lawler arrested the three men and transported them to the Four Courts Building. Prosecutors charged the three men with disposing of stolen property and running a business in an illegal manner.[xxxv]

Detective Desmond and Detective Lawler spent the day on

Friday, August 14, 1885, logging property into evidence. They also contacted the known victims to name their property. Based on their evidence, Emile Sasse and Son had to close their pawn shop until they resolved the case.

Desmond met one of the most famous international criminals in history, Eddie Guerin, in the mid-1880s. Guerin robbed the American Express Office in Paris in the early 1900s. French officials sent Guerin, a robber and thief to the French Guiana penal colony, Devil's Island.

Guerin became the first man to successfully escape from the prison in 1905. Guerin's six confederates died during the attempt but "the Fox" successfully made his escape.

Guerin's origins were obscure and "Three-Fingered Eddie" did all he could to keep it that way. Authorities believed Guerin grew up in Chicago, Illinois. Guerin may have been the wayward son of a wealthy family, but fact is hard to separate from fiction in Guerin's life.

Guerin committed his first notable robbery in Galesburg, Illinois as a 22-year-old. Guerin netted $10,000 in this heist.

Guerin also reportedly shot a police officer in Chicago. Saint Louis Detective Billy Desmond, the future Saint Louis Chief of Detectives, found Guerin to be non-violent and more intelligent than most criminals. Desmond took immense pride in having caught Guerin before Guerin robbed the Downtown Saint Louis Commercial Bank.

Figure 3-Mugshot of Eddie Guerin

Detective Desmond heard rumors that men came to Saint Louis planning to rob the Commercial Bank on Third Street. Detective Desmond and Sgt. Burke investigated the rumor. They caught Guerin and his crew casing the bank. Detective Desmond took Guerin and his accomplices to the Police Court, where the court gave the criminals hours to leave the city.[xxxvi]

In 1890, London Police caught Guerin during another bank robbery due to the incompetence of one of his accomplices. English authorities sentenced Guerin to Dartmoor Prison for 18 years. Guerin escaped and returned to the United States. Guerin intended to ply his criminal trade at the 1893 Chicago World's Fair.

At the Fair, Guerin met an infamous madame, Mary Anne "Chicago May" Churchill Sharpe. "Chicago May' was smitten with Guerin and began a long criminal and romantic association with the intelligent brigand. "Chicago May" supplied the money to help Guerin escape Devil's

Island. After the escape, Guerin and May had a falling out, when she took another lover. The couple shot at Guerin. The bullet wounded Guerin in the foot. Guerin quickly and permanently broke off his association with May.

Guerin's criminal career lasted until 1940, when he passed away at 80 years of age. Despite his record of big heists, Guerin died destitute. English authorities buried Guerin in a Manchester, England pauper's grave. Guerin never completely gave up his criminal ways.

Desmond continued catching criminals prior to the St. Louis Police Board appointing him St. Louis Chief of Detectives. During February 1890, Detective Desmond's persistent efforts to find two confidence men paid off with the arrest of both men.

"Kinch" Keegan and "Thatch" Grady were brothers-in-law and accomplices in confidence games. On January 24, 1890, the men tricked a Farmer Britt into giving them $18 as part of a check fraud at the Union Depot.[xxxvii]

Detective Lawler, who was acting Chief of Detectives while current Chief Hugh O'Neil's recovered from an illness, and his partner Detective William Desmond suspected Keegan and Grady of the crime. Britt confirmed their suspicions, when Britt picked Keegan out from the pictures of criminals kept by the Saint Louis Police.

The detectives believed both Keegan and Grady were lying low outside the city limits to prevent their arrest. However, Detective Desmond continued to frequent the areas known to be part of the crooks' normal haunts.

On the morning of Saturday, February 1, 1890, Detective Desmond found Keegan standing at the corner of Ninth and Olive Streets in Downtown Saint Louis.

Desmond arrested Keegan and took him directly to the Four Courts Building. Keegan was in custody for less than half an hour when his brother-in-law Grady showed up to inquire about his accomplice. Saint Louis Police promptly arrested Grady too.[xxxviii]

The First District Police Court judge accepted a charge of vagrancy against the men and continued the trial until February 5, 1890. The vagrancy charge was a technical one until Detective

Lawler could get Farmer Britt back to the city.^{xxxix}

Chief of Detectives Hugh O'Neil, who was sick from January 5, 1890, to February 23, 1890, returned to duty on February 24th. Desmond's partner and veteran detective, Pat Lawler supervised the department exceptionally well during the seven-week absence.

Chief O'Neil returned looking pale and haggard. Unfortunately, O'Neil never regained his full strength. On Tuesday, September 16, 1890, the Board of Police Commissioners appointed 33-year-old William Desmond to Saint Louis Chief of Detectives. Desmond served in this position for 17 years.

The board reduced Hugh O'Neil to Detective but placed O'Neil in charge of the Lafayette Park Station Detectives.

With William Desmond's promotion, the Saint Louis Metropolitan Police Department's detectives embarked on one of the most storied times in their history culminating with the protection of the Saint Louis World's Fair ground in 1904. Detectives like Chief of Detectives Hugh O'Neil and his old partner Pat Lawler helped to lay the road, which Desmond paved like few others.

Figure 4- Chief of Detectives William Desmond around the time of the 1904 World's Fair (Public Domain)

Chapter 3 – 33-Year-Old Chief of Detectives

In October 1890, Chief William Desmond's detectives solved their first big case. A bold string of night burglaries in the West End neighborhood caught the attention of the Saint Louis Police Chief.

The burglars broke into at least a dozen homes between June and October 1890. The burglars entered and stole items from the homes of two Saint Louis Police Officers, Officer McGrath and Officer McFarland.

Officer McFarland's son Terence grew up to be a Saint Louis Police Officer. A bank robber killed Terence in the line of duty during 1920.[xl]

Wealthy Saint Louisans lived

in the West End neighborhood, so the Mayor and Aldermen demanded the police solve the burglaries. On Thursday, October 2, 1890, the burglars cased a house, when Third District Officers noticed the burglars and stopped them for questioning.[xli]

The men, Paul Beyer and Julius Teunte, did not supply a clear answer for why they were in the area. The police officers searched both Beyer and Teunte. After finding burglary tools on both men, the police officers arrested Beyer and Teunte.

Detective Lawler and a couple officers searched Beyer's and Teunte's living quarters. Their search turned up dozens of items stolen in the earlier burglaries.[xlii]

Confronted with the evidence, both men confessed their

involvement in the burglaries to Chief Desmond.

Chief Desmond used his gift for conversation to wear down criminal suspects into talking to him. John Huey, an Indiana murderer, was not one of these cases. Huey freely spoke with Desmond about his criminal past. Huey escaped from Indiana after serving 13 years for a murder in 1874.

John Huey came to Lyon, Indiana in 1874 as a 22-year-old. Huey began hanging out with Elihu Hardin. By Huey's account, Hardin was a tough man who bullied others. On December 30, 1874, Hardin demanded that Huey buy him a drink or fight. When Huey took off his jacket to fight, Hardin pulled out a knife.

Huey fled the tavern and retrieved a firearm from his room. Huey said that he intended to leave town, but Hardin was waiting for him down the street. Hardin approached Huey with the knife. Despite Huey's pleas for Hardin to back off, Hardin continued to advance. Huey shot Hardin in the head. Hardin died instantly.[xliii]

Huey fled Lyon and lived in Terre Haute until arrested for Hardin's murder in 1876. In January 1877, prosecutors tried the case, but it ended in a hung jury. The prosecuting attorney dropped the murder charge in exchange for Huey's plea to manslaughter. In a surprise to everyone in the court room, the judge sentenced the 25-year-old Huey to 20 years in prison.

Huey later became a trustee. It was in this role that with only six months left before a parole hearing that Huey walked away from the Jeffersonville, Indiana prison during August 1890. The parole board intended to release Huey on parole. Huey worked in Southern Illinois before coming to visit his sisters in Saint Louis. Huey came to Saint Louis at the end of April and believed one of his relatives turned him in.

Detectives McGrath and O'Connell picked Huey up at his sister's residence near the intersection of Glasgow and Cass Avenues. Huey admitted his identity to them at once. They took him to speak to Chief Desmond at the Four Courts Building, where he told the above story.[xliv]

Huey returned to Indiana and served the rest of his term. Huey's congenial nature aside Huey refused to give up his criminal ways. Indiana officials arrested him and his brother Jack for theft in 1901.

The newspaper noted that the Hueys were known burglars.

Chief Desmond coaxed criminals into confessing to him over the years. While his contemporaries used techniques such as "the third degree" or beating prisoners, Desmond said violence was ineffective. Desmond got his results by talking to criminals.

He sometimes interrogated them like a drill instructor, but normally, he won their trust by treating them well and talking to them. Criminals contacted Desmond after they were in prison to supply him with information, an unheard-of accomplishment at the time.

Unlike other detectives, who sometimes used physical intimidation, Desmond eschewed the "third degree". Chief Desmond believed information obtained by beating suspects was completely useless.

Desmond started a discussion with the suspect. After putting him or her at ease, Desmond let the suspect talk freely. Desmond let them betray facts that exposed their crimes before asking a series of questions about what they discussed. Invariably, the suspects tripped themselves up with their lies. Soon the suspect confessed their part in the suspected crime(s).

On August 16, 1891, Saint Louis Police had Fred F. Osborne, a Billings, Montana resident, in prison for attempted fraud. After a discussion with Chief Desmond, Osborne went back to the Four Courts Building to sit in his cell and think. Within hours, he asked to see Chief Desmond again.

Osborne told Chief Desmond that he had recently fallen on tough times. While Osborne owned a small ranch in Montana, it was so heavily mortgaged, he could not sell it. Osborne had worked in Saint Louis two years earlier with the Northern Pacific Railroad. Before leaving for Montana, Osborne took bills of lading.

Osborne forged the bills of lading with the name of the Billings, Montana Station Agent. Osborne then wrote Downtown Saint Louis wool merchants about selling them $2,000 worth of wool. Osborne's inability to answer questions about wool made the merchants suspicious. Saint Louis Police arrested Osborne for attempted fraud.[xlv]

Osborne begged Chief Desmond to send him back to Billings where Montana would try him for forgery.

In Billings, he would at least be able to see his wife and three children. Despite the belief that Osborne was conspiring with a gang to defraud the merchants, Chief Desmond contacted the Billings, Montana authorities to see if they would prosecute Osborne for forgery. Chief Desmond intended to send him back to Montana if Montana was going to prosecute him.

On November 6, 1890, Chief of Detectives William Desmond brought in Pat Kennedy, a low-level Saint Louis crook. Desmond suspected Kennedy of stealing twenty cents from a cigar store on North 9th Street. A 3rd District Saint Louis Police Officer captured Kennedy after he robbed a Miss Minnie Mullaney at 16th Street and Franklin Avenue.

Kennedy proved a first-rate coward, who struck Miss Mullaney on the head from behind. As she lay dazed on the sidewalk, Kennedy pulled the purse from her arm and ran. Kennedy made off with $21 and jewelry of little value.

When the police seized Kennedy, he tried to tell a story but became confused and confessed his crimes. Kennedy's confession led to the arrest of his associate "Skinny" Woods. Woods helped Miss Mullaney up and acted like he was giving chase. However, he was only trying to catch up with Kennedy to split the loot.[xlvi]

After eating at a Downtown Saint Louis diner, the men threw the purse onto a roof at 12th and Wash, dumped the jewelry in a backyard and threw the purse in a sewer. Detectives Allendar and Burke recovered all the stolen property in the locations Kennedy specified.

The real spectacle occurred in Chief Desmond's office the next day. Desmond suspected Kennedy stole twenty cents from the cigar store of a blind man by the name of Louis Guibar on October 28, 1890. Detective McGuire brought Kennedy into Chief Desmond's office at the Four Courts Building.

When Kennedy entered the office, he spoke to Chief Desmond. "Good morning, Mr. Desmond." Mr. Guibar was sitting out of sight behind a door and sprung to his feet. "That is the man!"[xlvii]

Kennedy saw Mr. Guibar and said, "Yes, that is me, Mr. Guibar. I took the money from your drawer. I only got twenty cents, though, and I give ten of that back to McGurry."

McGurry worked for Mr. Guibar. McGurry saw Kennedy take the twenty cents. After Kennedy threatened to "bust his head", Kennedy gave McGurry ten cents out of the twenty he took.[xlviii]

McGurry named Kennedy as the man who stole the twenty cents. While twenty cents were not a large amount even in 1890, Mr. Guibar intended to prosecute Kennedy. Mr. Guibar said Kennedy was the head of the gang, who often stole from him when McGurry was running errands.

Chief Desmond said Mr. Guibar's identification was one of the most amazing things he saw in his long law enforcement career. Mr. Guibar only heard Kennedy's voice once or twice but was able to name him at once. Mr. Guibar could not explain his ability.

Chief Desmond arrested hundreds of criminals over the years, but seldom saw anything as remarkable as Mr. Guibar's identification of Pat Kennedy.

Over his 17-year career, Saint Louis Chief of Detectives William Desmond dealt with dozens of criminal's family members. Family members could be as bad or worse than the criminal Chief Desmond and his men had locked up. However, other family members were honest, diligent people, who struggled to understand what went wrong with their loved one.

Early in his career as Chief of Detectives, Chief Desmond heard a most unusual confession. In late February 1892, Chief Desmond's men arrested Patrick McAndrews for burglarizing a house.[xlix]

Figure 5- Chief Desmond interviewed non-criminals and talked to/comforted law-abiding family members of the criminals the St. Louis Police arrested (Public Domain)

Chief Desmond was familiar with the McAndrews family. Desmond knew them to be industrious parents with children in worthwhile occupations. However, police officers arrested Patrick on occasion for theft.

When Mrs. McAndrews came to visit her son, Chief Desmond gave permission for her to speak with Patrick. Mrs. McAndrews, well into middle age, spoke with her 20-something son for 30 minutes. Mrs. McAndrews burst into tears during their conversation.

After she finished speaking with Patrick, Mrs. McAndrews stopped in Chief Desmond's office to speak with him. Chief Desmond wanted to comfort Mrs. McAndrews and told her that Patrick must have picked up unpleasant habits by running with the wrong crowd.

Mrs. McAndrews told Chief Desmond, "No. It wasn't that." Mrs. McAndrews told Chief Desmond she saw a propensity in Patrick to steal items at an early age. None of Mrs. McAndrews other children stole or committed criminal acts. For this trait in Patrick, Mrs. McAndrews completely blamed herself.

Mrs. McAndrews related that prior to her son's birth, Mr. McAndrews had taken to drinking quite heavily. His drinking led him to be loose with the family's finances. Mrs. McAndrews struggled to pay for groceries and other household needs.[1]

To prevent her children from going hungry, Mrs. McAndrews began going through Mr. McAndrews pockets as he slept and taking the amount of money, she thought she could without

Mr. McAndrews discovering what she was doing.

By removing his money before he could spend it on alcohol, Mrs. McAndrews was able to get her family through this time. Mr. McAndrews quit drinking so heavily after a couple of months.

Mrs. McAndrews was pregnant with Patrick during this time. He was born a month or two after his father returned to his hardworking and thrifty ways. Mrs. McAndrews felt Patrick's propensity to steal was because she took Mr. McAndrews' money without his knowledge.[li]

Chief Desmond did not try to convince Mrs. McAndrews that taking money from her husband before Mr. McAndrews could spend it all and leave the family without food was different from burglarizing someone's home for ill-gotten gain.

Chief Desmond knew family members often blame themselves when a family member turns to crime. Trying to convince them it was not their fault often only increased their stress.

Chief Desmond thanked her for sharing her story with him and let her know that he was there to help her if he could. They parted amicably.[lii] I cannot find a record of Patrick McAndrews going to the Missouri Penitentiary, so hopefully he turned his life around after his arrest.

Figure 6-Artist Rendering of Business Owners Identifying Stolen Goods in Chief Desmond's Office During 1895 (Public Domain)

Chapter 4 – Frisco Train Robbery

Chief William Desmond solved his biggest case in his short career as Saint Louis Chief of Detectives in 1893. Daring train robbers held up the Frisco Train in September 1893.

On September 9, 1893, Frisco line brakeman James Pennock boarded the Frisco Line at Tower Grove in Saint Louis. At the Cheltenham stop, Frisco brakeman Sam Robertson and former brakeman Muncie Ray also boarded. The men boarded the train intending to rob the train at Sandy Cut, two miles east of Pacific, MO.

When the train got close to Sandy Cut, Muncie Ray and James Pennock climbed over the fuel car and demanded the engineers stop near Sandy Cut.[liii] After the men stopped the train, Ray and Pennock took them to the Express Car to burglarize the safe.

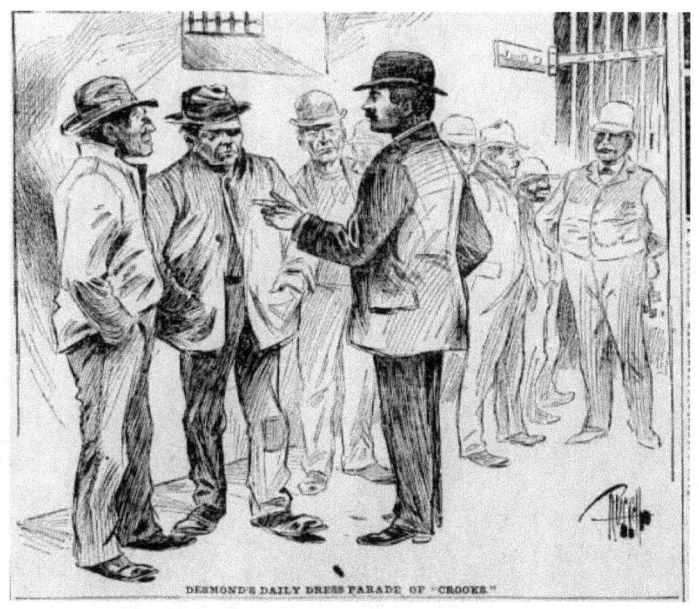

Figure 7- Chief Desmond interviewing arrested men in the holding cells of the Four Courts Building (Public Domain)

When Pennock knocked on the door, Express Messenger Campbell, who suspected nothing, opened the door. Campbell gasped as three armed men pointed pistols at him. However, Campbell recovered enough to the tell the men that the safe was empty.[liv]

Engineer Wickerly warned the robbers that another train was traveling down the same track. If Wickerly did not move the train, the other train would rear end the stopped train.

The robbers allowed Wickerly to start the train. The robbers decided they better take off while they had the chance.

As the three men started to make their escape, passengers from the approaching train and the conductor noticed the robbery.

Passenger Dr. Y.H. Bond loaded his shotgun, while Conductor Kerrigan pulled his own gun. Bond pointed his gun at Pennock, who separated from his accomplices.

Bond prepared to shoot Pennock, when Conductor Kerrigan

recognized Pennock, a brakeman on the same railroad. Kerrigan called Pennock over, where Kerrigan and Doctor Bond captured Pennock.[lv]

The railroad was not aware that Pennock already served a term in the Missouri Penitentiary for grand larceny in Crawford County. Pennock served his term between 1884 and 1886.[lvi]

Chief of Detectives William Desmond sent capable Saint Louis Police Detective Sam Allender to interview Pennock. All the CSI television shows lead people to believe scientific experiments and confronting the criminal with data and theory solves crimes. Skilled detectives talking to people solve crimes.

Allender sat in jail with Pennock all day engaging in small talk with Pennock. After Pennock started to trust Allender, he relayed the story of the robbery.

Pennock not only implicated himself, but Pennock also implicated Sam Robertson and Muncie Ray. Saint Louis Police arrested Sam Robertson, another Frisco Railroad brakeman, in Saint Louis at a house of prostitution at Sixth Street and Clark Avenue on September 7, 1893.

They captured Muncie Ray in Valley Park, Missouri on September 8, 1983. On the same day, the police arrested Ray, Chief Desmond and Detective Sam Allender gained a confession from Pennock and Robertson.

Sam Robertson originally denied his involvement. Pennock told him, "Come on, Sam. They got us dead to right."[lvii] Robertson contemplated this statement for minutes.

Robertson admitted being one of the three robbers. Robertson also admitted to shooting at the railroad men on both trains. The railroad workers shot at the fleeing robbers. Robertson returned fire.[lviii]

When Detective Allender prodded him, Robertson also confessed. He appeared relieved after his confession was complete.

On October 24, 1893, the Saint Louis Court sentenced James Pennock to the Missouri Penitentiary for 14 years for Robbery, 1st Degree. Pennock served over ten years. Prison officials released Pennock under the Three-Fourths Law on April 23, 1904.[lix]

Sam Robertson successfully petitioned for a change of venue, but the legal maneuver did not save Robertson from prison. The Gasconade County Court sentenced

Robertson to 15 years for Robbery, 1st Degree and Burglary, 1st Degree. Robertson served from December 15, 1893, to December 14, 1898. Acting Governor A. H. Bolt commuted Robertson's sentence.[lx]

Muncie Ray fled to escape the charges. He died a couple of years later in a streetcar accident in San Francisco, California.

The streetcar company employed Ray as a streetcar conductor. Another streetcar crashed into Ray's streetcar killing Ray.

Ray's death ended the case of the railroad robbery case. Desmond solved more high-profile cases, but the Frisco Train robbery is still one of his most famous cases.

Figure 8-Artist Rendering of a young Chief William Desmond

Chapter 5 – Capture of H.H. Holmes

Herman Webster Mudgett, who went by the alias Dr. Henry Howard Holmes, committed an undetermined number of murders during the 1893 Chicago World's Fair. H. H. Holmes was America's first known serial killer in the modern definition of the word. Holmes created "the Murder Castle", a Chicago hotel during the 1893 Chicago World's Fair.

Courts eventually convicted Holmes of sixteen murders, but Holmes may have murdered more than one hundred people during his operation of the hotel. What is less well known is that Saint Louis Police Chief of Detectives William Desmond supplied the information that led to Holmes' capture. Chief Desmond's treatment of criminals he interviewed led to the identification of H.H. Holmes.

Figure 9- H.H. Holmes, America's first serial killer (Public Domain)

Chief Desmond obtained the information due to his continuing contact with Marion Hedgepeth, a Missouri outlaw active in the western United States. Hedgepeth was born in Cooper County, Missouri during 1864. In 1882, Cooper County authorities arrested Hedgepeth for felonious assault.[lxi]

The Cooper County Court sent the 19-year-old Hedgepeth to the Boonville, Missouri reform camp in October 1882. After a year at the reform camp during October 1883, Hedgepeth escaped Boonville and stole a horse. Miller County officials captured Hedgepeth. They returned Hedgepeth to Cooper County.[lxii]

Governor Thomas Crittenden pardoned Hedgepeth for felonious assault in 1883, so the Cooper County Court could sentence Hedgepeth to the Missouri Penitentiary for stealing the horse and escaping Boonville.[lxiii]

The Cooper County Court sentenced Hedgepeth to four years in prison, but Hedgepeth served almost five and a half years meaning the court added time for other crimes Hedgepeth committed while in prison.[lxiv]

Hedgepeth entered the Missouri Penitentiary on November 19, 1883. Prison officials released him on February 16, 1889.[lxv] Hedgepeth headed west, where he continued his criminal career.

In 1891, Hedgepeth returned to Missouri. Hedgepeth and his gang of three other men robbed a train in the Glendale area of Saint Louis County on November 30, 1891.

Four men boarded the Saint Louis and San Francisco train as it stopped at the Old Orchard station. As the train approached Glendale, Missouri, two of the men covered their faces and climbed onto the locomotive.

The men pulled large revolvers on the engineers and fireman.

Normally, the train has one engineer and a fireman to run the train. However, another railroad engineer, George W. Jahrans rode in the locomotive as a passenger on the way home.[lxvi]

The robbers forced the train crew to stop at a particular spot on the rail tracks. The robbers then marched the train crew down the tracks to the express car.

Jahrans saw an opportunity to run and fled into the nearby woods. The smaller of the two robbers shot at Jahrans but missed. After the smaller robber shot at Jahrans, Jahrans heard a volley of shots.[lxvii]

The other two robbers exited the train, heard the shot, and mistook it for the signal. The two men fired a volley of shots into the roof of the smoking car. They were not trying to hit anyone. They simply wanted to cow the passengers and employees, so they would not interfere with the robbery.[lxviii]

As Jahrans hid in the woods, he heard an explosion as the robbers blew up the Adams Express Car. The explosion injured John Mutranen, the Adams Express messenger. Jahrans heard a second explosion when the robbers blew up the Express Car safe. The robbers fled with almost $75,000.[lxix]

Hedgepeth and his men met at 4244 Swan Avenue in the Forest Park Southeast neighborhood of Saint Louis to divide the money. The men then fled to California through Salt Lake City.

Desmond and his men found clues at the house, which was torn down before 1897. Desmond telegraphed a handful of Western police departments. Saint Louis Police brought Hedgepeth and Adelbert Slye to Saint Louis for trial in 1892.

Kansas Police shot and killed James S. "Jimmy Francis" in Pleasanton, Kansas on January 23, 1892. New York State prison authorities executed the further robber, Lucius P. "Dink" Wilson on May 14, 1894, at 12:32 p.m.[lxx] Wilson killed Syracuse Police Officer Harvey while trying to evade capture in 1892.

Chief Desmond obtained confessions from both Hedgepeth and Slye, who a Saint Louis Court convicted and sentenced to twenty-five years in the Missouri penitentiary.[lxxi] Chief Desmond kept a cordial acquaintance with Hedgepeth and Slye to gain more information about their activities. Marion Hedgepeth supplied more than Desmond ever expected.

Figure 10- Marion Hedgepeth at the time of his arrest in 1892 (Public Domain)

While Hedgepeth was in the Saint Louis jail for an appeal hearing, his cellmate was a house swindler named H. M. Howard. Howard approached Hedgepeth about an insurance swindle that he needed the services of a good local lawyer for and promised $500 to Hedgepeth for his help.[lxxii] This scheme eventually exposed Holmes and his earlier crimes. When Holmes did not pay Hedgepeth the agreed upon $500, Hedgepeth reported Holmes's conversation to Chief Desmond.

Figure 11- The infamous "Murder Castle", H.H. Holmes residence in Chicago during the 1893 World's Fair. Authorities found human remains but were unable to charge Holmes with any of the dozens of murders Holmes allegedly committed. Authorities executed Holmes for murders they could prove. (Public Domain)

Chief Desmond wired the Philadelphia Police, where Hedgepeth told Desmond that Holmes was travelling. Holmes and his victim, who thought he was part of the scheme instead of its victim, intended to claim the money in Philadelphia.[lxxiii]

Pinkerton detectives trailed Holmes to Philadelphia, where the Pinkertons arrested Holmes in 1894. Convicted of nine murders and five attempted murders, the state executed Holmes in Philadelphia on May 7, 1896.

For the information that he provided, Governor Joe Folk pardoned Hedgepeth in 1907 after serving 14 years of his 25-year sentence. Chief Desmond put in a good word for Hedgepeth with Governor Folk.

Like criminals before and since, Hedgepeth could not go straight. After serving a one-year sentence in Iowa for another robbery after his parole, Hedgepeth worked as a shoe salesperson for over a year in Minneapolis, Minnesota.

Hedgepeth seemed to tire of this life and travelled to Chicago, Illinois in late 1909.

On New Year's Eve 1909, Hedgepeth and Harry B. Featherstone, who was the heir to the title of Lord Featherstonhaugh in England, tried to rob Louis J. Novak's saloon at 3934 West Sixteenth Street.

Hedgepeth and Featherstone entered the saloon wearing bandanas over the face. Both Hedgepeth and Featherstone carried large revolvers, which they flourished as they ordered the customers, bartender, and Novak to hold up their hands.

Chicago Police Officer Henry G. Decker was passing the saloon, when Decker saw the eight men standing against the wall with their hands up. Decker burst into the saloon yelling at Hedgepeth and Featherstone," Up with your hands!"

Featherstone fired wildly at Decker but missed Decker with all six shots. Decker shot Featherstone, who fell to the floor.

Hedgepeth tried to help Featherstone, but bar patron Edward J. Burek knocked Hedgepeth to the ground. Hedgepeth jumped back to his feet and fled out the back door of the saloon.

Police Officer Decker and Burek chased Hedgepeth, who shot at both men as he fled. The gaunt Hedgepeth, who suffered from tuberculosis soon fatigued. Hedgepeth continued firing his gun. Decker returned fire and struck Hedgepeth in the head with one round.

An ambulance transported Hedgepeth to Saint Anthony's Hospital, where Hedgepeth died. Pinkerton detectives named Hedgepeth, who was using the alias "Albert Heywood," on January 3, 1910, two days after Hedgepeth died.

Hedgepeth was one of the fastest guns in the Old West circles, but age (45) and tuberculosis took its toll. Unknown parties interred Hedgepeth at Dunning Memorial Park in Chicago, Illinois.

Figure 12- Artist Rendering of Marion Hedgepeth (Public Domain)

Chapter 6 – Second Half of the 1890s

Chief Desmond made news by solving the Frisco Train Robbery and aiding in the identification of H.H. Holmes. Desmond still had other crimes to investigate in the second half of his first decade as Saint Louis Chief of Detectives.

During January 1896, an unnamed *St. Louis Post-Dispatch* reporter spent a week with Chief Desmond. The reporter came away with an interesting picture of a day in the life of the St. Louis Chief of Detectives.

Chief Desmond arrived in the office each morning no later than 8:30 am. Despite arriving early, Desmond did not leave before midnight. Sometimes, Desmond worked until 1 or 2 am.[lxxiv]

Chief Desmond checked in with St. Louis Police Chief Harrigan to start his day. After discussing the serious cases from the night before, Desmond went through his mail.

Chief Desmond checked the stolen property reports before assign cases to each of the detectives. Detectives remarked on Desmond's diligence.

After making the assignments, Desmond went down to the holding cells. Desmond started interviewing/sweating the men that detectives or patrol officers arrested the night before.[lxxv]

After the interviews, Chief Desmond and his assistant entered the information into the Bertillon System file for each suspect.

Chief Desmond then read all the newspaper stories about crime. After reading and marking the articles, Desmond started meeting with citizens. Visitors pleaded for their relative who was in police custody. Other visitors reported crimes.[lxxvi]

Chief Desmond ate dinner around 5 pm before returning to the office by 6:30 pm. Chief Desmond also made a tour of the Downtown pawn shops to check for stolen property.

Chief Desmond handed out assignments to the night detectives. Desmond also discussed their cases with the returning day detectives.

Desmond normally patrolled around Downtown for an hour or two before taking the streetcar home about midnight. Even if Desmond worked until 2 am, Desmond returned to the office by 8:30 am.[lxxvii]

Desmond kept up this schedule

even into his late forties. Desmond needed this determination to protect the city.

On December 3, 1896, three men entered the Home Brewery Office in Saint Louis at around 2:30 p.m. Cashier Robert Hofferkamp approached the men. The men produced revolvers telling Hofferkamp and his assistant to throw up their hands.

The men took $10,000 from the office, a multi-million-dollar heist today. The robbers tied up and gagged Hofferkamp and his assistant. Instead of fleeing the city though, the men stayed around Saint Louis. It was a big mistake on the men's part.

Saint Louis Chief of Detectives William Desmond worked his magic again. Desmond learned of the potential hiding place of the robbers. Desmond and East Saint Louis Police captured the three robbers, Joseph Stanley, Joseph McLaughlin, and Billy Wolf, on January 4, 1897, based on Chief Desmond's information.

Chief Desmond received a tip on the men's whereabouts from Stanley's lover. Desmond then personally arrested Stanley and McLaughlin in East Saint Louis, Illinois as they were trying to board a train for Indianapolis. Desmond sent detectives to pick up Billy Wolf, a local barber.[lxxviii]

In contrast to their bold heist, all three men quickly confessed to Desmond. They all admitted to their part in the robbery. While all three men served time in prison, I have not found any reference to the eventual outcome of the trial.

Billy Wolf continued to ply his trade in Saint Louis as a barber. He died in 1930 at 80 years of age after an automobile ran Wolf over. The Saint Louis Coroner could not decide whether someone killed Wolf, or an accident took his life. The coroner at least suspected the driver may have struck Wolf on purpose.

On February 10, 1897, 60-year-old William H. Stewart, a civil engineer, died in Saint Louis City Hospital. Stewart passed away from a morphine overdose.

Saint Louis Police originally thought it was a case of suicide or accidental overdose. Witnesses found Stewart unconscious at the rear of 1206 Washington Avenue.[lxxix]

Stewart lived with his son-in-law F.C. Bennett at 2634 Dickson Street. Mr. Bennett categorically denied Mr. Stewart used drugs of any kind. He also said Mr. Stewart had no reason to kill himself. Mr. Bennett suspected murder based on Mr. Stewart's missing jewelry consisting of a diamond ring, watch and chain. Mr. Stewart was also carrying cash.

Saint Louis Police Captain Joyce doubted foul play was involved. In fact, Joyce was furious that the St. Louis Coroner ruled Mr. Stewart's death a murder.[lxxx]

Saint Louis Chief of Detectives William Desmond was concerned about the missing property. Desmond sent Detectives Badger and Freese to check the local pawn shops. On February 16, 1897, the detectives found the jewelry in a pawn shop.

Saint Louis Police arrested a local rooming house owner, Charles

Griffo, for pawning the watch. Detective O'Connell arrested a second man, Hiram Brooks, who admitted to pawning the missing ring for Griffo. Police arrested Miranda Griffo, Charles' wife, as an accomplice.

Chief Desmond sweated all three suspects over Stewart's death. Griffo and his wife told Desmond that two girls, Bertha Nixon and Lizzie Henry, brought Stewart to their rooming house. Nixon and Henry rented a room from the Griffos at 1203 Washington Avenue.

Nixon and Henry lured Mr. Stewart to the house to spike his drink with "knockout drops". After Stewart fell asleep, Nixon and Henry planned to rob Stewart of his valuables. While Henry was entertaining Stewart, Nixon slipped the drops into a drink she prepared for Stewart. The concoction was too strong for Stewart, who quit breathing.

Not sure if Stewart was going to recover or die, the women summoned Charles Griffo. Griffo and Hiram Brooks carried Stewart to the rear of 1205 Washington Avenue, where they left Stewart. A Saint Louis Police Officer found Stewart, but Stewart died at the Saint Louis City Hospital.

Griffo and Brooks pawned Stewart's property for a split of the proceeds. Lizzie Henry travelled to Toledo, Ohio to stay with family. Bertha Nixon moved to another rooming house run by the Griffos, who also moved their residence. After Griffo and Brooks confessed, Saint Louis Police arrested Bertha Nixon.

Chief Desmond sent a dispatch to Toledo Police, who arrested Henry. After Saint Louis Police brought Henry back from Toledo, Desmond interviewed both women. Nixon and Henry both confessed to the murder but said it was accidental. The knockout drops were only supposed to make Stewart lose consciousness.

During May 1897, prosecutors presented their case against Nixon and Henry for murder in Judge Zachritz's court room. Zachritz told the jurors they could consider manslaughter if they thought Henry and Nixon killed Stewart accidentally. The jury found them guilty of manslaughter. Zachritz sentenced both to 2 years in prison for Stewart's murder.

18-year-old Bertha Nixon served about eighteen months from

July 11, 1897, to December 8, 1898. 28-year-old Lizzie Henry served about the same time from July 14, 1897, to November 28, 1898.

If Chief Desmond had not sent the detectives to the pawn shops, they would not have discovered the murder. Thanks to Chief Desmond's instincts, the Saint Louis Police solved the murder.

Figure 13- Chief Desmond display burglary tools seized by the Saint Louis Police (Public Domain)

Chapter 7 – Ten Years as Chief

In 1900, Chief Desmond had served as Chief of Detectives for ten years. In the previous ten years, Desmond built a nation-wide reputation.

On Monday, March 5, 1900, Saint Louis Police Officers Thomas Meagher and Thomas Degnan arrested two men. During the following investigation, the officers discovered Ed Sullivan, a 22-year-old transient, robbed an East Saint Louis Police Officer of his gun, jewelry, and possessions in late February 1900.[lxxxi]

Officer Meagher of the Central District was patrolling his beat when he saw Sullivan and Harry Davis walking near Olive and Fourth Streets. When the men saw Officer

Meagher, they tried to "slink off" according to the March 6, 1900, *Saint Louis Republic*. Officer Meagher ordered Sullivan and Davis to halt. It almost cost Meagher his life.[lxxxii]

If Officer Meagher had searched Sullivan first, Sullivan could not have shot him. Meagher searched Davis first. While Meagher searched Davis, Ed Sullivan pulled a .38 caliber revolver from his shirt and shot Meagher through the shoulder.

Sullivan and Davis fled as Meagher, although seriously wounded, fired his service revolver at them. Meagher started chasing Sullivan and Davis. Officer Degnan was at Second and Locust Streets when Degnan heard the shots.

Running towards Olive on Third Street, Degnan ran directly into

Sullivan and Davis at the corner of Third and Olive. All three men were surprised but Degnan quickly knocked the gun from Sullivan's hand with his night stick.

Sullivan put up his fists to fight but a single strike to the head from Degnan's night stick subdued Sullivan. Private Watchman Frank McTigue had been walking with Degnan and pulled his revolver on Davis who surrendered without a fight.

Even though the shooting seriously injured Officer Meagher, Meagher insisted on walking the men to the call box at Third Street and Washington Avenue. After a patrol wagon picked up Sullivan and Davis, Meagher rested at the neighboring firehouse. An ambulance took Meagher to City Hospital for treatment.

Chief of Detectives William Desmond questioned Ed Sullivan, who admitted to robbing East Saint Louis Sergeant Cooney, a private security guard and another man over the past months. Sullivan refused to implicate Davis in any of these crimes. Davis claimed to be from Toronto, Canada and only visiting Saint Louis.

Officer Meagher survived the shooting and worked himself up to Special Officer by 1905. Officer Meagher was the officer who discovered the American Tent and Awning Fire that took the lives of Saint Louis Firemen.[lxxxiii]

Officer Meagher was born on March 9, 1868. He spent his 34th birthday recovering from a bullet wound at his home on North Ninth Street.

Figure 14- Chief Desmond respected the gentlemen skilled criminals he arrested (Public Domain)

While this case was routine, Chief Desmond gave the *St. Louis Republic* an interview about Desmond's famous cases during the summer of 1900.

For the Sunday, June 24, 1900, edition of the *Saint Louis Republic*, a reporter interviewed Saint Louis Chief of Detectives William Desmond about the increasing violence of the new criminal. After 10 years as Saint Louis Chief of Detectives, Chief Desmond lamented the increasing violence he was seeing out of the "hobo burglar".[lxxxiv]

Chief Desmond told the reporter that when he was a young detective, he took immense pride in catching the old school professional burglar. Chief Desmond cited their intelligence and gentlemanly ways, when not involved in criminal activities, as the noted characteristics. Desmond said old school criminals did not resort to violence but surrendered before shedding blood.

Chief Desmond singled out "Big" John Wilson, Eddie Guerin, Colonel Parker, and Henry Watson as burglars of the old school. "Big" John Wilson was an Irish boiler maker. A well-spoken man, who mixed well with people, Wilson stole diamonds from a Downtown Shop. The proprietors never could figure out how Wilson took them.[lxxxv]

Eddie Guerin took bank notes from the bank counter, while a confederate distracted the teller. After getting out of the Missouri penitentiary, Guerin plied the same trade in England and Germany before French police caught him.

Henry "Nip" Watson specialized in relieving actors of diamonds. Chief Desmond said Watson was one of the handsomest and best dressed men in Saint Louis. For a long time, no one in Saint Louis society realized Watson made a living as a burglar and thief.

Chief Desmond had the most respect for a confidence man from Texas, Colonel Parker. In the early 1880s, Colonel Parker convinced Saint Louis businesspeople that Parker had a large herd of cattle headed to the stockyards in East Saint Louis, Illinois. Chief Desmond was a young detective at the time.

Saint Louis businesspeople bid against each other for Colonel Parker's business. After Parker stayed in Saint Louis for months, but no cattle showed up, the men began to ask Parker questions. Figuring the investors had discovered his scheme, Colonel Parker skipped out of his hotel with the hotel's silverware.

Detective Desmond and his partner caught Colonel Parker in a small Illinois town. After the detectives brought Parker back to Saint Louis, the Colonel contracted an illness. Despite an ambulance taking him to City Hospital, Colonel Parker quickly deteriorated and passed away. Chief Desmond sounded almost thankful that Colonel Parker escaped prison.

Chief Desmond expressed a harsher view of the new school criminals. Chief Desmond resented the daring but unintelligent new school criminals' violent ways.[lxxxvi]

Figure 15-Violent, daring but unskilled criminals that Desmond despised (Public Domain)

Chief Desmond said most "new school criminals" began their careers by running away from home. After being on the street for a while, Chief Desmond felt most were beyond reform. Characterizing them as hungry half the time and drunk the other half, Chief Desmond described them as unskilled criminals, who often bungled their jobs but fought like wild men to escape capture.

John Joyce alias Scut Crane was the first hobo criminal to work in Saint Louis around 1885. Joyce sat around the saloons. When Joyce saw a man with money, Joyce encouraged the man to get intoxicated. Joyce then offered to escort the man safely home. When Joyce and his victim came to a dark alley, Joyce clubbed the victim with a Billy, cleaned out his pockets and left the victim in the gutter. It took the Saint Louis Police months to catch Joyce.

Thomas Stockton committed similar crimes. At the time of the story in the *Saint Louis Republic* on June 24, 1900, Stockton was serving his fourth term in the Chester, Illinois penitentiary. The last time the Saint Louis Police arrested him, Stockton had only been out of the penitentiary two days. Stockton fought two detectives in a saloon on Sixth and Pine Streets. The detectives eventually bashed Stockton into submission. The Saint Louis Police sent Stockton back to the Missouri penitentiary in the same suit they released him.

Saint Louis Police found Elmer E. Fuller in a doorway on Pine Street during a storm. Fuller had been trying to pry open a lock. Fuller acted innocent and refused to talk "to protect a lady's reputation".

During a search, Saint Louis Police found a gun on Fuller. After a week of investigating, Chief Desmond discovered Fuller broke out of a Kansas jail. Saint Louis Police returned Fuller to the Lansing, Kansas penitentiary to serve his sentence.

Chief Desmond singled out William "Saint Paul Tip" Thornton as one of the worst of the hobo criminals. Thornton murdered Officer Nicholas Hunt after robbing a Downtown establishment in 1897.

Desmond still considered Thornton a boy in age and temperament. Despite coming from a good family in New Orleans, Thornton ran away to San Francisco, where Thornton began his criminal career.

During his time in Saint Louis, Thornton organized a group of young burglars and robbers. While Thornton's gang poorly planned their crimes, the short but strong Thornton escaped arrest by quickly resorting to fists or firearms.

Thornton shot Officer Hunt when Hunt almost ran into Thornton, who was fleeing his most recent robbery.[lxxxvii]

Officer Hunt was neither the first nor last officer to run into a criminal fleeing the scene of a crime. Chief Desmond himself ran into a fleeing criminal in fall 1900. On Monday, October 15, 1900, Chief Desmond seized the pants of a thief but not the thief himself.

Jonas Washington entered the yard of Shickle, Harrison and Howard Iron Foundry at 12th and Gratiot Streets around 5 pm. Washington began to load his two-horse wagon with a ton of steel castings. It was normal for drivers to pick up material in this way. Washington went about his work with such boldness that Washington escaped attention.

Foundry clerk David Young noticed Washington and approached Washington about loading his wagon. Washington told Young that he was loading the wagon to take it to the scales which was the normal process for picking up materials. Young went back to his office.

A minute later, Young looked out his window and saw Washington heading for the 12th Street Viaduct. Young began to pursue Washington, but Washington whipped the horses to full speed and left Young behind. Young told Saint Louis Patrolman Con Hough of the Central Police District about the theft.

Patrol Officer Hough joined about fifty foundry employees in pursuing Washington through the streets on streetcars and buggies. Washington abandoned his cart in front of the Four Courts Building, headquarters to Saint Louis Police and Courts, at 12th and Clark Streets.

Washington ran into a restaurant and vaulted two tables to escape Saint Louis Police Detective Tom Walsh. Washington ran into the new City Hall, down through the basement and exited out onto Market Street. Saint Louis Chief of Detectives William Desmond was traveling home in his buggy. Desmond gave Roscoe Shaw, Chief Campbell's stenographer, a ride to Shaw's home.[lxxxviii]

Desmond and Shaw saw the pursuit of Washington and joined in the pursuit. Pursuing Washington into Center Street where Washington tried to climb a fence, Desmond alighted from his buggy. Desmond grabbed Washington by his pant leg and started to pull Washington back from the fence.

Washington slipped out of his pants and dropped to the other side of the fence. Roscoe Shaw, who jumped the fence while Desmond had Washington by the pants leg, wrapped Washington up in a bear hug. Other officers arrived and took Washington into custody.

Washington had already served a prison term for theft in Illinois under the name John Doyle. Washington received three years for this theft. In 1905, Washington received a pardon from Governor Joseph "Holy Joe" Folk, but Washington returned to prison shortly after his pardon.[lxxxix]

Saint Louis Detective Evans arrested Washington for theft of scrap metal. Chief Desmond had the Circuit Attorney charge Washington as a persistent offender. Desmond ended up with both his trousers and his man.

Because Saint Louis was the largest city west of the Mississippi River, pickpockets and thieves rode the rails to ply their illicit trade in the bustling metropolis. On September 21, 1901, hotel employees overpowered a sneak thief, who tried to burglarize a room in the plush Southern Hotel.

Charles Forrest was not a run of the mill thief. Forrest entered the Southern Hotel at 5 am in a Prince Albert coat, pressed pants, and silk hat. Forrest casually walked up to the third floor.

Forrest carefully made sure no one saw him before Forrest checked all the doors. Forrest hit the jackpot at the room rented by

Charles E. Wilson, a traveling salesperson from New York.

Charles Wilson was sleeping in his room, but the bold Forrest entered anyway. Wilson was a New York traveling salesperson in Saint Louis for a convention. Forrest removed $16 in cash, a watch, and gold pin from Wilson's clothing hanging over a chair.

Wilson started to stir so Forrest dropped to the floor by the bed. Wilson almost went back to sleep but decided to stand up and check on the noise. Wilson stepped down on Forrest's leg, while Forrest was trying to hide under the bed.

Forrest rose to his feet and wrestled with Wilson for a couple of minutes. Forrest freed himself from Wilson's grip and fled with Wilson in hot pursuit.

Porter William Meehan and Bell Boy John Spangler pounced on Forrest. Forrest tried to wrestle with Meehan and Spangler, but their profession gave them better-than-average strength. Meehan and Spangler flopped Forrest on his face and held Forrest there until Saint Louis Police Officer Flaherty arrived.

Saint Louis Chief of Detectives William Desmond interviewed Forrest, who confessed to the attempted burglary. Forrest claimed to be from Omaha. Desmond believed Forrest was from Chicago, where the tailors of Forrest's jacket ran their business. Forrest's jacket had the name W.T. Carroll on the label.

Forrest claimed the burglary was his first offense in Saint Louis. Forrest did not claim it was his first criminal act though. Forrest's actions gave him away as a bold and practiced sneak thief.[xc]

Desmond and his men caught bigger fish in November 1901. In doing so, Desmond met one of the toughest criminals Desmond ever "sweated."

On Tuesday, November 5, 1901, Saint Louis Police captured Ben Kilpatrick and Laura Bullion for their part in the Great Northern train robbery in Montana on July 2, 1901. It took weeks for the police to discover who they captured.

In the first week of November, a well-built man, who was interested in buying a watch, approached a Saint Louis jeweler. The jeweler sold him the watch for $85, which the mysterious man paid for with new $20 bills drawn on the Bank of Montana. The man left with the watch and the jeweler went to deposit the considerable sum at the bank.

Figure 16 - Ben Kilpatrick with other members of the Wild Bunch (Public Domain)

The bank refused the deposit from the jeweler, Max Barnett of the Globe Loan Company at 109 N. Sixth Street, because the cash matched the description of the bills stolen in the Great Northern Train Robbery. The jeweler notified Chief of Police Kiely.[xci]

Kiely had a secret weapon at his disposal, "The Sherlock Holmes of Saint Louis", Chief of Detectives

William Desmond. The 44-year-old Desmond put four of his best men on the case. While a couple of them were making inquiries, they saw a man matching the description of the shopper walking Downtown. At 6 feet tall and two hundred pounds, the police easily spotted the stranger.

The detectives watched him enter 2005 Chestnut Street before they called for aid. Once the reinforcements arrived, Detectives John McGrath, Al Guilon, John Shevlin, George Williams, James Burke, and Will Brady made the arrest. Detective Guilon set up the arrest by acting like a drunken man who was looking for his room.

Guilon stumbled into the man's room. Guilon asked why the stranger was in "his room". When "John Arnold", the name he gave Saint Louis Police, stood up to protest and escort Guilon out of the room, the other detectives poured in. Guilon quickly took the powerful stranger down and secured his right arm, which was reaching for a revolver. Detective McGrath quickly grabbed his left arm and removed a second revolver that "Arnold" was reaching for.[xcii]

Detectives found $483 on "Arnold" and the gold watch which he bought from the Globe Loan Company. The money was fresh twenty-dollar bills drawn from the Bank of Montana. Saint Louis Police captured Arnold's companion "Lillie Rose" as she returned to the room. The police recovered $7,000 of the stolen money in her suitcase.

"Lillie Rose" quickly admitted her real name was Laura Bullion. Bullion was a known associate of the Wild Bunch. The detectives believed their man was Harvey Logan also known as Kid Curry. They were not correct in this identification.

Figure 17- Prison photo of Laura Bullion (Public Domain)

The case also shows that law enforcement was not sure about the true identities of the Wild Bunch. The police thought Harvey Logan and Harry Longbaugh were the same person. Longbaugh was the famous "Sundance Kid". The Saint Louis Police also thought Butch Cassidy had been in Saint Louis with

"Arnold". Butch Cassidy and "The Sundance Kid" moved their operations to South America in February 1901. The other accomplice in Saint Louis was most likely Harvey Logan.

While Chief Kiely interviewed Bullion, Detective Chief Desmond interviewed "John Arnold" who turned out to be Ben Kilpatrick. Kilpatrick, a Texas cowboy, took part in Wild Bunch robberies under the leadership of Butch Cassidy and later Harvey Logan.

Chief Desmond always said that Kilpatrick was one of the toughest interviewees that he ever had. It took weeks of "sweating" Kilpatrick before Kilpatrick gave Desmond the most basic information. Kilpatrick eventually admitted his part in the robbery but did not implicate anyone else.[xciii] He served 10 years of a 15-

year sentence in the Missouri Penitentiary.

Kirkpatrick did not remain free long. Police shot Kilpatrick during a robbery in Memphis, Tennessee on March 12, 1912, nine months after the Missouri parole board released Kilpatrick from the Missouri Penitentiary. Kilpatrick was dead at thirty-eight.[xciv]

Laura Bullion served three and half years of a five-year sentence. The state released her in 1905. She continued moving around the country until she settled in Memphis in 1918. She spent her later life as a mender and housekeeper. She died in Memphis on December 2, 1961, at the age of eighty-five.

The salacious details of Chief Desmond's next high profile case shocked St. Louisans. Police investigated a wealthy Saint

Louisan found dead in a bath house.

On Thursday, January 23, 1902, Saint Louis awakened to the news that a bath house attendant found millionaire A. Deane Cooper in the Vista Bathhouse at Franklin Avenue and North Grand Boulevard with a severe head wound. Cooper, one of Saint Louis' wealthiest men, owned residential real estate and other assets valued at two million dollars.[xcv]

Cooper aspired to be the biggest property owner in Saint Louis. Cooper may have achieved his goal if not for his premature death at 49-years-of-age.

On Wednesday, January 22, 1902, Cooper arrived at the Vista Bathhouse, which Cooper owned. After Cooper suffered an attack of apoplexy in 1901, Cooper bought the bathhouse to take regular Turkish baths. William Strother aka William Straugher attended Cooper. Cooper had a close relationship with Strother, which was unusual in turn of the century Saint Louis. Strother was both poor and black. Cooper was wealthy and white.

After Cooper arrived, Strother heated up the sauna for Cooper. After a steam bath in the sauna, Cooper returned to the cooling room, where Cooper had a cot. Cooper told Strother he was expecting a man and two women to visit him at the Turkish bath. Cooper said one of the women was having an affair with him but due to her prejudice she did not want any Black people around her.

Strother agreed to stay out of sight, but Cooper told Strother that Strother could peek in the bathhouse after Strother saw the agreed upon signal from Cooper. The newspapers covered this aspect of the crime cautiously, because Cooper arranged for Strother to be able to peek in at the naked white women, who often joined Cooper at the bathhouse.

Strother peeked in on them after receiving the signal from Cooper. Strother returned around midnight to find everyone gone. He saw Cooper lying on a cot. When Strother checked on his employer, Strother found Cooper insensible from a strike to the head. Strother summoned Cooper's son, Theodore Cooper, and the Saint Louis Police.[xcvi]

In a case of this significance, Chief of Detectives William Desmond, personally managed the investigation. The police quickly found the murder weapon, a sledgehammer with blood stains, in a stack of coal underneath the

Turkish bath in the basement.

Figure 18- Chief Desmond sweating William Strother (Public Domain)

Chief Desmond quickly focused on the three visitors and William Strother. Strother's alibi crumbled quickly. Under a series of "sweatings", the term Desmond used for his interrogations, Desmond progressively got confessions from Strother.

Strother admitted taking Cooper's missing jewels, that Strother brought the murder weapon up out of the basement, that Strother hid the sledgehammer in the basement and finally that Strother struck Cooper with the fatal blow.

Desmond never discovered a clear motive. Strother attempted to hide the jewelry, so robbery could have been the motive. Cooper had also recently bought the house that Strother lived in. Despite Cooper's promises that Cooper was going to redeem the house for Strother, Strother feared Cooper was going to take Strother out of his house. Cooper bought Strother's house during the week of January 22, 1902.[xcvii]

Figure 19- Artist Rendering of William Strother at the time of Cooper's murder (Public Domain)

Besides, his lover, A. Deane Cooper, had a dark side. Cooper allegedly bankrolled the operation of Saint Louis gambler Johnny Winn. Cooper asked Winn to have one of Cooper's co-workers "slugged". Cooper hoped his employers would think the co-worker was keeping bad company and fire the man.

Cooper's dual life may have led to the hung jury at Strother's first trial. Strother quickly pled guilty to Second Degree Murder during jury selection for his second trial. The Saint Louis Court sentenced Strother to a 15-year sentence from which the state released him early for good behavior. The state released Strother on September 9, 1913. He lived less than a year.

On July 25, 1914, 52-year-old William Strother died in the City Hospital. Strother died because of lung disease. Strother was working as a lead miner. Strother was homeless at the time of his death. The city buried Strother in the Potter's Field.

At the end of 1902, St. Louis Police investigated another interesting case. On Friday night, October 24, 1902, an informer passed information to Assistant Chief of Detectives James Smith.

A stranger in town placed an order with S. J. Schultze & Co., a Saint Louis printing firm, to print checks for the Elgin City Banking Company of Elgin, Illinois. The informant doubted the stranger worked for the Elgin Bank.

Assistant Chief Smith detailed Saint Louis Detective John Keeley to stake out the company. Keeley selected Saint Louis Police Special Officer Thomas McNeil to help him on the surveillance. Keeley and McNeil waited only a brief time. Around 11 a.m. on Saturday, October 25, 1902, a slight built man arrived at the printing company and claimed the package.

Keeley and McNeil began to follow the stranger, who soon realized someone was following him. As Keeley moved closer to the man, the stranger suddenly turned and threw the package in his face. The man began to flee down Olive Street in Downtown Saint Louis.

The stranger first ran through the Jesse French Plano Company at 1116 Olive Street. The man's actions terrified women shoppers as the man tried to pull a revolver from his waist.

As the stranger and the pursuing officers exited the store, the man freed the revolver and fired two shots at Keeley but missed with both. Keeley and McNeil returned fire, which convinced the man to run faster.

Scared people are capable of abnormal feats. The fleeing suspect jumped a ten-foot ditch, which briefly allowed him to put distance between himself and the pursuing Saint Louis Police Officers.

The man ran through a rooming house on Chestnut Street, but the police officers showed great endurance by gaining on the man. All three men ran through a second house on Chestnut terrifying three women inside.

Bystanders including John Pearsall, the superintendent of the Saint Louis Health Department horses and vehicles, joined in the chase. Pearsall was able to trip the unlucky crook. Keeley and McNeil jumped on the man and took his pistol. The stranger tried to fight but repeated blows to the man's head subdued him.

At first, the man refused to admit anything or supply his name to police. Eventually, he confessed he was William Smith, a forger. Smith had four aliases and served two prison terms in both New York and Missouri. Smith intended to use the fake checks in a Texas forgery scheme.

At his hotel room, Saint Louis Police arrested a young lady, who was typing letters to send to Texas along with the fake checks. The police also seized a bag with two large pistols and considerable ammunition. Smith wore a cartridge belt around his waist.[xcviii]

Saint Louis Police initially charged Smith with attempted murder for shooting at Keeley. However, Saint Louis Chief of Detectives William Desmond and Circuit Attorney Joseph "Holy Joe" Folk intended to charge Smith as a habitual offender, which carried a potential life sentence.

Chief Desmond investigated violent crime throughout his career. In December 1903, safe burglars conducted a brutal crime.

On December 15, 1903, at about 2:00 o'clock in the morning, George Harding, the clerk of the Erie Hotel, was busy working in his office. Used to working alone, Harding had relaxed his vigil and did not notice three large, hard looking men enter the hotel at Fourth and Clark Streets.

The first man entered Harding office with a drawn revolver. The robber told Harding to raise his hands. The sudden appearance of the man startled Harding, but Harding quickly raised his hands.

While the first man held Harding at gunpoint, the other two men began to break into the safe. The armed man signaled to his confederates that he heard someone coming down the hall. Victor Dawson, the Erie Hotel's cook, and one of the few employees in the hotel was walking to the clerk's office.

The robber trying to break into the safe was using a sledgehammer. The robber slid his frame behind the door to shield himself from Dawson's view. As soon as Dawson entered the room, the desperado brought the sledgehammer down on Dawson's head. Dawson dropped at once, where his assailant struck him with two or three more blows. The cowardly attack killed Dawson.

As the men fled the building, the armed man shot Harding. The owner estimated that the robbers took $300 from his safe. For months, Saint Louis Police had no leads.[xcix]

However, Saint Louis Detectives Cremins and Finan got a tip that taxi driver Willis E. Hall, alias "Louis Heavy", may have been involved in the robbery. Cremins and Finan began tailing Hall relentlessly.

In early April 1904, Saint Louis Chief of Detectives William Desmond ordered his men to pick up Hall. They arrested Hall at 4301 Easton Avenue, his home residence, early in the morning on April 12, 1904. Hall was a tough customer but no match for Chief Desmond, who talked countless criminals into confessions over the years.

Feeling "the third degree" did not produce true information, Desmond used a clever way of questioning and interacting with the suspect to induce them to confess. Desmond seldom failed in getting the guilty man to admit his crimes.

Hall quickly revealed that the robbery crew was Hall, James Duffy, and Charles Stevens. They planned the robbery on December 14, 1903, in a saloon at the corner of Eighth and Walnut Streets. Hall refused to admit shooting Harding, but Hall was the only one with a firearm. Duffy was the assailant, who killed Dawson with the sledgehammer.

Charles Stevens was already serving an eight-year sentence for another robbery in the Missouri Penitentiary. The police never caught James Duffy.

When Willis Hall came before Judge Turner, Hall decided to plead guilty rather than face trial and a death sentence. Judge Turner sentenced him to 99 years in prison.[c] Governor Elliot Major pardoned Willis Hall on December 24, 1913.

Solving the Erie Hotel robbery was a feather in the cap for the Saint Louis Police Department but nothing unusual in the storied career of Chief William Desmond.

Figure 20- Willis Hall (Public Domain)

Chapter 8 – Boodling Case and New Assistant

In 1903, Chief Desmond appointed a new assistant, spent time in Mexico trying to extradite a high-profile Saint Louis political figure and got married for the first and only time in his life.

On Monday, December 15, 1902, Saint Louis Police Assistant Chief of Detectives James H. Smith retired from the police department to take a position in the coal industry. Chief of Detectives William Desmond tried to convince Smith to stay but Smith decided to retire from the force as his fortieth birthday approached.

Smith compiled a commendable record as Desmond's Assistant. The Saint Louis Police Department appointed Smith as a police officer on April 16, 1889, when Smith was 26 years old. The Police Board appointed Smith to detective in 1892. The Board appointed Smith to serve as Assistant Chief of Detectives in 1899.

James H. Smith prospered in the coal business and owned a private residence on Newberry Terrace in the Lewis Place neighborhood. Born on February 13, 1863, Smith lived to be 72 years old. Smith passed away from heart failure on August 19, 1935.

John J. Keely was 29 years old and a Saint Louis Police Clerk, when the board appointed him an officer with the department on March 20, 1895. The Police Board appointed Keely to detective on December 6, 1898.

On June 28, 1900, Dan Julian and "Biddy" Holden shot Detective

Keely, who was trying to arrest them over a shooting affray Downtown. Shot four times, Keely was in critical condition for days in Saint John's Hospital before Keely pulled through.

John Keely assumed the duties of Assistant Chief of Detectives on January 1, 1903. He held the position until 1907, when Keely took over as Chief of Detectives from his friend and mentor William Desmond.

John J. Keely took his new position at a salary of $1800 a year. Keely continued to protect Saint Louis until retiring to a home in the 5900 block of DeGiverville Avenue. Built in 1912, the home still stands today. Keely was born on November 4, 1864. He passed away after a battle with cancer on April 20, 1939, at 74 years of age.

Besides gaining a new assistant, Chief Desmond made major news with a change in his personal life.

On January 7, 1903, Saint Louis Chief of Detectives William Desmond married 24-year-old Hannah McLaughlin in a ceremony he hoped to keep secret. The 46-year-old Desmond always said he would never marry due to the dangers of his job. However, Desmond was clearly smitten with Hannah McLaughlin.

Chief Desmond always worried about the dangers of his job and the possibility that Desmond would leave Hannah a young widow. As the World's Fair approached in 1904, Desmond's worries compounded.

For the 1904 World's Fair, the Saint Louis Police Department divided in two. Chief of Police Mathew Kiely commanded the uniformed force and focused on policing the city. Chief Desmond and his detectives supplied security and investigated crimes at the World's Fair. Officers from around the country and private officers like the Jefferson Guard at the World's Fair supplemented Chief Desmond's force.

Besides the 1904 World's Fair, Joe Folk's boodling investigation put a crimp in Chief Desmond's domestic happiness.

During his boodling investigation, Saint Louis Circuit Attorney Joseph "Holy Joe" Folk indicted City Councilman Charles Kratz for taking bribes or "boodle" for his vote on certain bills. Kratz claimed innocence but took the curious step of fleeing Saint Louis for Guadalajara, Mexico.

Figure 21- Charles Kratz in 1902 (Public Domain)

Mexican authorities arrested Kratz on April 28, 1902, but the extradition took considerable time.[ci] Kratz exercised every legal tactic he could to prevent Mexican authorities extraditing him back to the United States.

The United States and Mexico were also not at a high point of their relationship. The process drug out for almost two years between 1902 and early 1904.

Chief Desmond traveled to Mexico three times before Desmond secured Kratz's return to the United States. Desmond's first trip to Mexico in 1902 lasted two months. He made the 5,488-mile round trip to lay the groundwork for Kratz's eventual return.

Chief Desmond's second trip only lasted two weeks but circumstances forced him to make the trip one more time. By the time Chief Desmond returned to Saint Louis with Kratz, Desmond logged 16,464 miles over three trips.

Desmond also spent three months in Mexico during 1903.

Finally on January 9, 1904, Mexican officials turned Kratz over to Chief Desmond and Saint Louis Sheriff Dickmann, who made the last trip with Desmond. Chief Desmond felt relieved after the entered U.S. territory on the train bringing them back to Saint Louis.[cii]

A legal maneuver foiled all the effort spent bringing Charles Kratz back to Saint Louis. In 1904, Kratz secured a change of venue to Butler County, Missouri. After illness delayed his trial repeatedly, a Butler County jury needed less than two hours to return a verdict of "Not Guilty" in Kratz's case.

Kratz was one of the final defendants in the "boodling investigation". Unlike the other defendants, Kratz escaped conviction. The investigation ended the career of Saint Louis' elite like "Boss" Ed Butler, the head of St. Louis' Democratic machine.

For Chief Desmond, his involvement with the case ended with Kratz's return to Saint Louis. Desmond quickly had to switch gears and prepare his army of detectives for the challenge of protecting the Fair during Saint Louis's crowded hour. Chief Desmond could find no time to rest.

Figure 22- Colonel Edward "Boss" Butler from the Public Domain

Chapter 9 – 1904 World's Fair

Chief Desmond took on his toughest assignment in 1904 when he assumed responsibility for policing the World's Fair. The Louisiana Purchase Exhibition, or 1904 Saint Louis World's Fair as it is more popularly known, is the most significant event in Saint Louis, Missouri history. While Saint Louis was the largest city west of the Mississippi River, the World's Fair put it on the international map. While the fair brought notoriety, tourists, and increased revenue to the city, it also brought criminals. Criminals nationwide traveled to the "Gateway to the West" to profit from the Fair.

Standing in the breech to meet this criminal band was the experienced Saint Louis Chief of

Detectives William Desmond. Chief Desmond needed all his skills to deal with the pickpockets, robbers and thieves that made Saint Louis a stopping point during the 1904 World's Fair.

The World's Fair opened on April 30, 1904. Before the Fair closed, Chief Desmond and his men arrested five hundred criminals. Chief Desmond "sweated" or interrogated 318 of these criminals. Saint Louis Police sent the rest to other states where the arrested person was facing criminal charges from earlier crimes. Saint Louis Police took other criminals to the train station and made them leave on the first available train.

Detectives from other departments aided Chief Desmond's regular contingent of detectives. The Saint Louis Police Department granted these special officers a commission to serve during the World's Fair. Two of the special officers were helping in the arrest of the Alton train robbers in October 1904. This arrest led to the death of three Saint Louis police detectives and two of the train robbers.

Criminal sometimes succeeded in their shady doings, but Chief Desmond and his men kept the criminal class in check. As the newspaper articles noted at the time, criminals left town to tell their criminal associates "Stay away from Saint Louis and DESMOND!"

During the Fair, "The Thief Taker's" normal force of fifty-four men doubled to one hundred local detectives plus detectives from around the world. Scotland Yard even sent two men to Saint Louis.[ciii]

On May 17, 1904, Saint Louis Detective Frank McKenna and Hummell proved their efficiency. While making their rounds at the Hotel Jefferson, Hummell called out, "Hello, Rufus." Rufus Woods was shocked.

Woods was known throughout the United States as a diamond and hotel thief. Woods tried to play it off by saying, "I beg your pardon, gentlemen. You seem to have the advantage of me." McKenna and Hummell had the advantage as they took Woods into custody and transported Woods to the Four Courts Building.

When they arrived with Woods at the Four Courts, Chief Desmond took Woods into his office. Desmond had McKenna and Hummell search the prisoner. The detectives found opium in capsule form as well as two diamonds removed from their mountings.

Woods claimed the diamonds came from a theft he committed in San Francisco. During his "sweating" from Chief Desmond, Woods admitted to serving a penitentiary sentence in Toronto, Canada. Police also arrested Woods at the Pan-American Exhibition in Buffalo, New York in 1901.

Woods normally collaborated with a female confederate. Chief Desmond sent out a directive to his men to be on the lookout for the female thief. Woods was not going anywhere soon.[civ]

Chief Desmond sweated another dangerous criminal during October 1904. Desmond did not know it, but the explosives expert was part of the crew which robbed the Alton

Pacific train earlier in 1904. The robbery had a tragic culmination.

On Friday, October 21, 1904, one of the deadliest shootings in Saint Louis Police history occurred when two train robbers and three Saint Louis Police detectives died in a shootout. The gunfight occurred in a small hotel room on Pine Street.

Two days later, Sunday, October 23, 1904, a burglar tried to gain entry to a realty office at 612 Chestnut Street by dropping a bottle of nitroglycerin on the sidewalk. If not for the first incident, police may never have discovered the identity of the perpetrator of the second deed.

The explosion at Samuel Bowman and Co. was so destructive that citizens heard it ten blocks away. The nitroglycerin injured the burglar as well. "John Doe" suffered a broken foot, a disintegrated pants leg and scratches on his face and body.

Doe tried to escape but his damaged leg made it impossible. Police Officer Tom Quinn ran from his beat on Seventh and Chestnut Streets to catch Doe trying to run into the alley. Doe had a .45 caliber revolver in his waistband.

Doe looked to be about 30 years old but claimed to be "John Doe, 23, shoemaker, single, no home." Doe's proclamation before any police questioning betrayed his knowledge of police interrogation methods. Doe refused to make any other statements.

Saint Louis Police Chief of Detectives William Desmond faced tough interviews in his day. Desmond "sweated" suspects in a friendly but disorienting interrogation style. Even the normally reticent Ben Kilpatrick eventually talked to Desmond. Doe was proving an exception.

Unfortunately for Doe, Saint Louis Police captured train robber Harry Vaughn outside the Pine Street Hotel where the gunfight occurred. Vaughn faced a long sentence for his role in the train robbery, so Vaugh was looking for ways to reduce his sentence.

Vaughn sent for Desmond and told Desmond that John Doe was Jerry Franklin Ferguson. Ferguson was a member of their gang specializing in bank robbery and business burglary. Faced with Desmond's knowledge of his identity, Ferguson admitted his name but continued to refuse to divulge any knowledge or complicity in the explosion.

During the first week of November 1904, Ferguson's former girlfriend Agnes Blanc, who earlier lived with Ferguson, exposed Ferguson as a member of Vaughn's gang. Blanc implicated Ferguson in the train robbery and reported that Ferguson was one of the eight prisoners who escaped the Neosho, Missouri Jail in 1903. Neosho Sheriff's Deputies caught Ferguson after Ferguson blew up a store safe.

Ferguson was looking for Blanc and her new boyfriend who Ferguson intended to kill with the explosives instead of robbing the realty office. When a drunk Ferguson dropped the bottle and seriously injured himself, Ferguson's injury spared the couple.

Faced with this overwhelming evidence, Ferguson finally confessed to Chief Desmond. Desmond sent Ferguson back to Neosho to face the burglary charges.[cv] Eventually, I lose track of Ferguson.

Before Chief Desmond completed his assignment at the World's Fair, Chief Desmond dealt with an unexpected personal tragedy.

Figure 23- Chief Desmond during the 1904 World's Fair (Public Domain)

Chapter 10 – Tragedy Visits Desmond

Before Desmond took responsibility for safeguarding the Fair, 45-year-old William Demond married 24-year-old Hannah McLaughlin at St. Ann's Catholic Church on Wednesday, January 7, 1903.[cvi]

Despite Desmond's best efforts, friends found out about Desmond's impending marriage and leaked the information to the Saint Louis newspapers. Desmond surprised his friends because Desmond vowed not to marry because of the dangers he faced daily as St. Louis Chief of Detectives.

Hannah McLaughlin caught Chief Desmond's eye in 1897 when she was eighteen and Desmond was forty. The *St. Louis Post-Dispatch* carried an announcement about Desmond's upcoming marriage to McLaughlin.[cvii] However, Desmond told the newspapers that he and Hannah were only close friends. When they did not marry, friends figured Desmond intended to remain a bachelor.

Other officers and police officials kidded and teased Desmond about his bachelor status from his earliest days as a detective. Despite the ribbing, Desmond did not show any interest in marriage.[cviii]

Criminals said Desmond always caught his man. Hannah McLaughlin showed the same determination. Hannah refused to show interest in other suitors. Hannah said she would marry Desmond or no one.

Finally, Desmond could resist no longer and married Hannah. Reverand O. J. McDonald of St. Ann Catholic Church married the Desmonds at St. Ann Catholic Church in a private ceremony.

Robert Jenks, chief clerk of the St. Louis Fire Department served as best man for Chief Desmond. Maria Desmond, Chief Desmond's younger sister, served as maid of honor.[cix]

Chief Desmond and his new wife headed to San Francisco for a twenty-day tour of the West Coast. Desmond promised to stop in at the San Francisco Police Department to pass on the good wishes of the St. Louis Department.

Despite their difference in age, Chief Desmond and Hannah Desmond had a happy marriage. However, the union would not last long.

Chief and Hannah Desmond found out after their honeymoon that Hannah was pregnant. Hannah gave birth twins, who both died. Hannah took the twins death particularly hard.^{cx}

Despite their loss, they tried for another child soon after and Hannah gave birth to a son, William Desmond, Jr. in June 1904. Baby William was a healthy baby, but Hannah fell ill during William's birth.

Despite around the clock nursing care, Hannah did not show any improvement over the next eight weeks. On Sunday morning, August 14, 1904, at 5:50 am, Hannah McLaughlin died at the Desmond home, 4290 Page Avenue. Hannah's death devastated Chief Desmond.^{cxi}

Despite William Desmond's heartbreak, Chief Desmond continued working. Two months after Hannah's death, the Alton Train Robbers shot and killed three of Desmond's detectives in a tiny rooming house in Downtown St. Louis. The officers killed the robbers also. It was the deadliest shootout in St. Louis Police history.[cxii]

Marie Desmond moved in with Chief Desmond to help her brother with William, Jr. Maria served as the only mother William, Jr. would know. Chief Desmond had to find a way to go on.

When William Desmond married Hannah, Desmond could not have imagined that he would outlive Hannah. In fact, Hannah took more of a risk that she would be a young widow. With a 21-year difference in age and Chief Desmond's dangerous occupation, the life insurance tables would predict Hannah long outliving Chief Desmond.

William and Hannah Desmond took a chance but had a happy, if short, marriage. Had they not taken the chance, they would not have enjoyed two happy years before Hannah passed away. It is hard not to celebrate their courage in striving for happiness.

Figure 24- Hannah McLaughlin Desmond in 1903 (Public Domain)

Chapter 11 – Lord Barrington

Thief. Liar. Bigamist. Con Man. Murderer. All correct labels for one of the greatest charlatans to work in Saint Louis. "Lord F. Seymour Barrington" was a bit of a local celebrity, if an extremely disreputable one, during 1903. After conducting a bigamist marriage on the East Coast, "Lord Barrington" stole his wife's trousseau and headed to Saint Louis.

When Barrington arrived in Saint Louis, Barrington quickly set out to find another wife to set himself up locally. Barrington found a target in the intelligent but inexperienced Wilhelmina Grace Cochrane of Kansas City, Missouri. Barrington made the acquaintance of

Miss Cochrane's sister and brother-in-law.

During Barrington's visits to their home, Barrington impressed Miss Cochrane with tales of his English estate. After a brief courtship, Miss Cochrane became Mrs. Barrington during January 1903.[cxiii]

Mrs. Barrington's brother was suspicious of Lord Barrington's story and began looking into his background. Mr. Cochrane discovered that his sister was Barrington's third wife. "Lord Barrington" did not bother divorcing either of his first two wives.

"Lord Barrington" under his real name Frederick George Barton, a graduate of Dartmoor prison not Oxford University, married Celestine Elizabeth Miller in Brooklyn. When they left for

England, English police arrested Barton and returned him to Dartmoor for an earlier prison escape. Barton never contacted Mrs. Barton or their child when Barton returned to the United States.

During his second trip to the United States, Barton moved to Philadelphia. In Philadelphia, he posed as "Lord Frederick Sydnham Burgoyne". Barton married a young woman on December 1, 1902, a mere six weeks before he married Miss Cochrane. On December 23, 1902, "Lord Burgoyne" abandoned his new wife and made his way to Saint Louis as Lord Barrington.

When Mrs. Barrington's brother realized that "Lord Barrington" had tricked his younger sister into a bigamist marriage, Mr. Cochrane traveled from Kansas City to Saint Louis to confront his new brother-in-law. The confrontation occurred at his sister, Mrs. Elliot's, home at 4368 West Belle Place.

Mr. Cochrane, an athletic young man in his mid-twenties, confronted Barton aka Barrington with what he had discovered. "Lord Barrington" decided the best defense was a good offense and hurled insults at Mr. Cochrane. Mr. Cochrane responded with a strong punch to Barrington's nose.

As "Lord Barrington" tried to regain his composure, Mr. Cochrane grabbed Barrington by the collar, expelled Barrington from the house and continued striking Barrington with his fists. As they got to the sidewalk, Mr. Cochrane placed a solid foot into "his Lordship's" backside with a strong command to leave and never come back.[cxiv]

Figure 25- Frederick George Barton alias F. Seymour Barrington in court for bigamy (Public Domain)

Alerted by "Lord Barrington's" cry for help, two Saint Louis Police Officers responded to the scene. To Barrington's dismay, the officers arrested him for a large, unsettled bill at the Southern Hotel. "Lord Barrington" aka Frederick Barton returned to the familiar haunts of jail for the next couple of months in the Saint Louis Workhouse.

Mr. Cochrane took his sister back to Kansas City. Mrs. Barrington in an interview with the Saint Louis Post-Dispatch said she "hated him (Lord Barrington)." This marriage of Barton's ended in divorce when Mrs. Barrington divorced Barton to become Miss Cochrane again.

While Lord Barrington served months for defrauding the hotel, Barrington had just begun his Saint Louis criminal career. Saint Louis

Police had not seen the last of "Lord Barrington".

On June 26, 1903, St. Louis Detectives Cordell and Schmidt arrested Barrington on minor charges. However, Chief Desmond and his men were investigating the disappearance of James P. McCann.

McCann met Barrington in a local tavern not long after the St. Louis Workhouse officials released Barrington on fraud charges. Barrington's financial prospects had not improved. McCann told Barrington that Barrington could stay with McCann and McCann's wife until Barrington was in a better financial position.[cxv]

Barrington told Chief Desmond that on Thursday, June 18, 1903, McCann and Barrington left the McCann home at 2902 Franklin Avenue.

The men took a train out to Suburban Park in St. Louis County.

Barrington said that he and McCann met up with two unidentified men and a woman. McCann knew the woman, who led McCann away from the group for privacy. Five minutes later, the woman screamed. The two men ran and attacked McCann.

Barrington came to McCann's aid but one of the men knocked Barrington unconscious. When Barrington came to, McCann asked Barrington for any money that Barrington was carrying. Barrington gave McCann $27.50.

McCann, who Barrington said was drunk during the entire incident, started to leave in a carriage with the two unidentified men and the woman. Barrington tried to convince McCann not to leave with group, but McCann insisted.

One of the men kicked Barrington into the gutter, where Barrington lay insensible until about 4 am on June 19th. Barrington took the train back to the McCann home, where Barrington told a similar story to Mrs. McCann.[cxvi]

Chief Desmond did not believe Barrington's story, but a lack of evidence forced Desmond to release Barrington. Barrington's run of luck ended the following day, Saturday, June 27, 1903.

A farmer living near Bonfils Station in St. Louis County reported a body floating in an abandoned quarry. The quarry was two hundred yards from the St. Louis, St. Charles, and Western Railroad stop that Barrington and McCann left on the night of June 18, 1903.[cxvii]

Figure 26- The McCanns and Barrington in happier times (Public Domain)

The train conductors found it odd that Barrington and McCann left the train at such a secluded spot. The train had not left when the conductors heard one of the men scream followed by two to three gunshots.

Once the St. Louis County Coroner joined the team of St. Louis City Police Officers to make the search outside of the city limits legal, the officers recovered not only McCann's body but found his clothes scattered hundreds of yards apart trying to prevent identification.

Chief Desmond had detectives arrest Barrington just in time as Barrington was preparing to leave Saint Louis. Saint Louis Police discovered a pistol, which was the same caliber as the gun used to kill McCann.

After transporting Barrington back to the Four Courts building, the arresting officers inspected the police carriage they used to convey Barrington back to Chief

Desmond's office. The officers found two pieces of James McCann's jewelry, which Barrington tried to hide in the seat.[cxviii]

Mrs. McCann had one of her household staff deliver Barrington's clothes, which Barrington wore on the morning Barrington returned after McCann's disappearance. Mrs. McCann did not believe Barrington's story, so she had one of the household staff seize the clothes before Barrington destroyed them.

Chief Desmond found blood on the clothing. Barrington refused to admit to murdering McCann but did admit being near the area, where the farmer found McCann's body.[cxix]

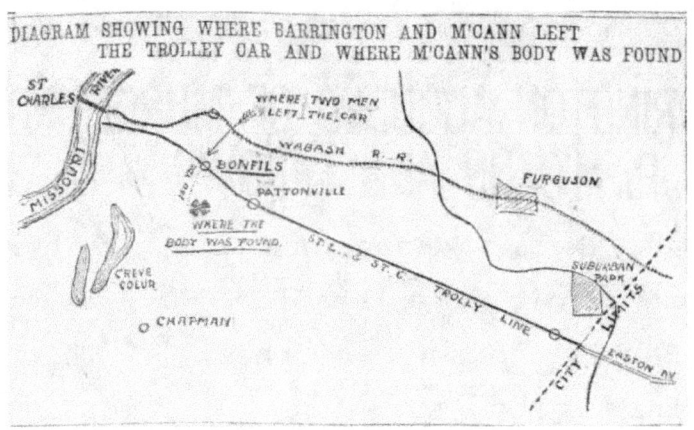

Figure 27- Map of the McCann Murder Scene (Public Domain)

Chief Desmond took Barrington to the scene of the crime. Barrington did not show any emotions as they inspected the murder scene. Barrington did admit the story about the women was not true.

Newspaper reporters found it hard to believe that Barrington could kill McCann, who was bigger than Barrington because Barrington was effeminate, cowardly, and a cur. Desmond agreed that Barrington was effeminate and a coward but disagreed that Barrington could not kill McCann. Desmond felt a coward like Barrington would only try to kill McCann in a secluded location with a firearm.[cxx]

In November 1903, Barrington went on a hunger strike because he did not find the St. Louis County Jail food to be edible. The hunger strike lasted days.

In February 1904, St. Louis County tried Barrington for murder. After a two-week trial, the jury convicted Barrington for murder. The judge sentenced Barrington to hang.

Barrington and his attorneys appealed the verdict to the Missouri Supreme Court. In August 1907, Governor Joe Folk commuted Barrington's death sentence to life in prison. Barrington served his sentence in the Missouri penitentiary from August 28, 1907, to December 24, 1918. Governor Dockery commuted Barrington's sentence after eleven years in prison.[cxxi]

As part of Barrington's parole, Barrington had to leave the United States within sixty days or go back to prison.[cxxii] Barrington returned to England.

About the time that Folk commuted Barrington's sentence, Folk's Police Board would change Chief Desmond's life in a way Saint Louis could never imagine.

Figure 28- Barton aka Barrington awaiting trial in St. Louis County (Public Domain)

Chapter 12 – Travesty of Justice

In January 1907, the Board of Police Commissioners perpetrated a great injustice for the city and department. "For the good of the department". With those six words, the Saint Louis Board of Police Commissioners removed Saint Louis Chief of Detectives William Desmond from the position Desmond held for 17 years. The Board replaced Desmond with Desmond's ex-assistant James Smith, who the earlier board dismissed from the police department.

How did one of the greatest, if not the greatest, detectives in Saint Louis Police history with an impeccable reputation for honesty end up so ignobly demoted in an unfair action that shortly led to his retirement? The dismissal was political and had its origins in the "boodling" investigation of 1902-1904.

Joseph W. "Holy Joe" Folk served as an attorney during the 1900 Saint Louis Streetcar Strike. Folk was disgusted by the tactics of the Saint Louis' business elite during the strike. After voters elected Folk as Saint Louis Circuit Attorney, Folk started investigating corruption between businesspeople and Saint Louis politicians.

Folk felt the Saint Louis Police hindered Folk's corruption investigation. Folk intended to get even with the office through the Police Board as the governor appointed the members of Saint Louis Board of Police Commissioners.

The Board of Police Commissioners seated during the

"boodling" investigations was not friendly to Folk and his investigation. The Board members often interfered by giving contradictory orders to individual police officers, who the earlier board summoned through the Saint Louis Police command staff.

However, Chief Desmond ignored the board and worked with "Holy Joe". Desmond personally traveled to Mexico and brought back one of the city legislators, who fled there to escape prosecution in 1902. Desmond brought the man back despite preparing for his upcoming wedding in January 1904.

When Folk won the Missouri Governor's race in 1905 based on his record as Circuit Attorney, Folk addressed the interference of the Board of Police Commissioners in his earlier investigation. It took Folk a year and a half, but Folk replaced enough Board of Police Commission members with his own appointees to remake the department.

Not satisfied with removing the Police Commissioners, who obstructed him, Folk ordered his appointees to remove anyone Folk saw as interfering with his investigation. Folk's puritan zeal brought Desmond into the crosshairs of the new board.

The Board of Police Commissioners ordered Desmond to remove 15 to 20 detectives, who the Board believed interfered with the "boodling" investigation or were corrupt. Desmond did not agree with the Board's assessment. Chief Kiely also told Desmond not to remove any detective Desmond was not convinced were corrupt.

Neither Kiely nor Desmond felt the board should fire a rank-and-file officer for following orders from the earlier Board of Police Commissioners. The Board could bring the men up on charges and have the officers dismissed. If they did not take money for their actions, Chief Kiely and Chief Desmond said the board should not fire the officers. Despite their long records including bringing Saint Louis safely through the 1904 World's Fair, their failure to scapegoat the officers led to Kiely's and Desmond's dismissal.

The Board of Police Commissioners first asked Chief Mathew Kiely for his resignation. At first, they were slow to do the same to Chief Desmond. On January 21, 1907, the Board met and planned to ask for Desmond's resignation.

However, a public outcry led them to leave him in his position. The board intended to remove him in September 1907, when his reappointment was due.

Four days later, after Folk changed their mind, the Board of Police Commissioners requested Desmond's resignation. Desmond resigned as Chief of Detectives and the board reassigned him to the rank of Lieutenant.[cxxiii] The Board intended to promote him to Captain, which it did before he resigned months later. This unfair and ignominious end to his career haunted Desmond for the rest of his life.

As it turned out, losing Desmond was not "for the good of the department". Chief Desmond's resignation hurt the department. Lucky for Saint Louis, the Police

Board railroaded Desmond after the 1904 World's Fair, where Desmond oversaw the police and security operation in an exemplary manner.

Figure 29- Ex-Chief William Desmond and New Chief James Smith (Public Domain)

Conclusion

On Tuesday, July 4, 1916, former Saint Louis Chief of Detectives William Desmond passed away after an illness of two years. Desmond was in Alexian Brothers Hospital from October 1915 until his death on Independence Day 1916. The 59-year-old Desmond left a 12-year-old son, William Desmond, Jr. Chief Desmond's wife died ten years before him.

For 17 years from 1890 to 1907, William Desmond led the Saint Louis Detective's Bureau during one of its most successful eras before and after the 1904 World's Fair. Desmond's men managed policing the World's Fair.

While still a detective, Desmond was known for his fighting

ability. One winter night, Desmond tried to arrest a man on the ice-covered streets at Third and Christy Streets. After a lengthy battle, Desmond and his prisoner staggered into the Third District Station. Half frozen and showing the damage from their battle, the man said he wanted no more of the battered but triumphant Desmond.

Criminals may fear a tussle with Billy Desmond, but it was his mind which made him truly dangerous to the criminal element. Chief Desmond's real skill was "sweating" suspects. Unlike the third degree or physical abuse in practice at the time, Desmond gained confessions through clever questioning and understanding the criminal mind.

Desmond first suggested a reason like self-defense for the crime. As the suspect talked about the crime, Desmond showed him or her that self-defense really was not possible but supplied another reason for the criminal's actions. The criminal then confessed to key facts. By the end of the interview, Desmond normally had a full account of the crime and a confession.

Chief Desmond left the force in 1907 but felt the Stewart Police Board forced him out for political reasons. Desmond was bitter over how his retirement occurred. He carried this bitterness until his death from pneumonia on July 4, 1916. From 1907 until 1915, Chief Desmond ran a private detective agency with one of his former assistants, John Keely.

The funeral procession began at his home, 4290 Page Boulevard, and ended at Saint Ann Catholic Church. Miss Maria Desmond, who lived with her brother and his son, continued to take care of her nephew after her brother's death.[cxxiv]

Chief Desmond's death closed for good the career of the greatest thief taker in Saint Louis Police history. The Future Chief of Detectives found Chief Desmond a tough act to follow.

Figure 30- Chief Desmond in his later years (Public Domain)

Other Saint Louis History and True Crime Books

Deadly Decades: St. Louis Police Tales from 1910 to 1927

True Crime, Disasters and Police Tales of Old St. Louis

The Union Missouri Bank Robbery

The Jobbing of Andrew J. Gordon: The St. Louis Police's First Black Detective

Shootout on Pine Street: The Illinois Central Train Robbery and Aftermath

St. Louis Civil War: The Streetcar Strike of 1900

2912 Washington and the Murder of Arthur Huddleston

Bibliography

Newspapers

Bloomfield Vindicator (Bloomfield, Missouri)

The Chattanooga Daily Times (Chattanooga, Tennessee)

Golden City Herald (Golden City, Missouri)

Leavenworth Tribune (Leavenworth, Kansas)

The Missouri Republican (St. Louis, Missouri)

Mexico Weekly Ledger (Mexico, Missouri)

St. Louis Globe-Democrat (St. Louis, Missouri)

St. Louis Post-Dispatch (St. Louis, Missouri)

St. Louis Republic (St. Louis, Missouri)

St. Louis Star and Times (St. Louis, Missouri)

The Washington Times (Washington, D.C.

Books

Shootout on Pine Street by Ken Zimmerman Jr. Saint Louis: Ken Zimmerman Jr. Enterprises, 2014.

Websites

Missouri Death Certificate Database. www.sos.mo.gov

Missouri Penitentiary Records Database. www.sos.mo.gov

About the Author

Ken Zimmerman Jr. is a married father and grandfather, who lives outside of Saint Louis, Missouri. Ken fell in love with Saint Louis history listening to his grandparents, Gilbert and Alvina Ellis, talk about Old Saint Louis.

If you like this book, you can

sign up for Ken's newsletter to receive information about future book releases. You can sign up for the newsletter and receive a bonus e-book by going to www.kenzimmermanjr.com.

Endnote

Introduction
[i] St. Louis Post-Dispatch, January 10, 1890, p. 5
[ii] St. Louis Post-Dispatch, July 5, 1916, p. 1
[iii] St. Louis Post-Dispatch, October 22, 1878, p. 4
[iv] St. Louis Post-Dispatch, July 2, 1881, p. 6
[v] St. Louis Post-Dispatch, October 26, 1881, p. 6

Chapter 1
[vi] St. Louis Post-Dispatch, August 11, 1881, p. 8
[vii] Ibid
[viii] Missouri Penitentiary Database, Spencer H. Davis and William H. Anderson
[ix] Ibid
[x] St. Louis Post-Dispatch, August 4, 1882, p. 8
[xi] Ibid
[xii] Ibid
[xiii] Missouri Penitentiary Database, Alexander Estes Record
[xiv] Ibid
[xv] St. Louis Post-Dispatch, February 13, 1883, p. 4
[xvi] Ibid
[xvii] Ibid
[xviii] Ibid
[xix] Ibid
[xx] Ibid
[xxi] Ibid
[xxii] Leavenworth Tribune (Leavenworth, Kansas), April 4, 1883, p. 4
[xxiii] St. Louis Post-Dispatch, August 9, 1883, p. 8
[xxiv] Ibid
[xxv] St. Louis Post-Dispatch, December 26, 1884, p. 5
[xxvi] Ibid
[xxvii] Ibid
[xxviii] St. Louis Post-Dispatch, December 27, 1884, p. 7
[xxix] Ibid
[xxx] Ibid, p. 2

[xxxi] St. Louis Post-Dispatch, January 2, 1885, p. 5

Chapter 2
[xxxii] St. Louis Post-Dispatch, July 8, 1885, p. 7
[xxxiii] Ibid
[xxxiv] St. Louis Post-Dispatch, August 15, 1885, p. 2
[xxxv] Ibid
[xxxvi] St. Louis Post-Dispatch, September 5, 1888, p.3
[xxxvii] St, Louis Post-Dispatch, February 1, 1890, p. 6
[xxxviii] Ibid
[xxxix] Ibid

Chapter 3
[xl] 1920: The Deadliest Year for St. Louis Police by this author
[xli] St. Louis Post-Dispatch, October 3, 1890, p. 2
[xlii] Ibid
[xliii] St. Louis Post-Dispatch, May 11, 1891, p. 4
[xliv] Ibid
[xlv] St. Louis Post-Dispatch, August 16, 1891, p. 4
[xlvi] St. Louis Post-Dispatch, November 6, 1890, p. 5
[xlvii] Ibid
[xlviii] Ibid
[xlix] St. Louis Post-Dispatch, February 28, 1892, p. 7
[l] Ibid
[li] Ibid
[lii] Ibid

Chapter 4
[liii] St. Louis Post-Dispatch, September 6, 1893, p. 1
[liv] Ibid
[lv] Ibid
[lvi] Missouri State Penitentiary Records for James Pennock
[lvii] St. Louis Post-Dispatch, September 8, 1893, p. 1
[lviii] Ibid
[lix] Missouri State Penitentiary Record for James Pennock

[lx] Missouri State Penitentiary Record for Sam Robertson

Chapter 5
[lxi] Golden City Herald (Golden City, Missouri), November 1, 1883, p.2
[lxii] Ibid
[lxiii] Bloomfield Vindicator (Bloomfield, Missouri), November 24, 1883, p. 1
[lxiv] Missouri State Penitentiary for Marion C. Hedgepeth
[lxv] Ibid
[lxvi] St. Louis Globe-Democrat, December 2, 1891, p. 9
[lxvii] Ibid
[lxviii][lxviii] Ibid
[lxix] Ibid
[lxx] St. Louis Post-Dispatch, May 14, 1894, p. 1
[lxxi] Missouri State Penitentiary Record for Marion C. Hedgepeth
[lxxii][lxxii] St. Louis Post-Dispatch, November 20, 1894, p. 1
[lxxiii] Ibid

Chapter 6
[lxxiv] St. Louis Post-Dispatch, January 12, 1896, p. 29
[lxxv] Ibid
[lxxvi] Ibid
[lxxvii] Ibid
[lxxviii] St. Louis Post-Dispatch, January 5, 1897, p. 1
[lxxix] St. Louis Post-Dispatch, February 11, 1897, p. 6
[lxxx] St. Louis Post-Dispatch, February 13, 1897, p. 5

Chapter 7
[lxxxi] St. Louis Post-Dispatch, March 7, 1900, p. 4
[lxxxii] St. Louis Republic, March 6, 1900, p. 1
[lxxxii] Ibid
[lxxxii] St. Louis Republic, June 24, 1900, p. 34
[lxxxii] Ibid
[lxxxii] Ibid
[lxxxii] Ibid

lxxxii St. Louis Republic, October 16, 1900, p. 3
lxxxii Missouri State Penitentiary Records
lxxxii St. Louis Post-Dispatch, September 22, 1901, p. 1
lxxxii St. Louis Republic, November 6, 1901, p. 1
lxxxii Ibid
lxxxii St. Louis Post-Dispatch, November 15, 1901, p. 1
lxxxii The Chattanooga Daily Times, March 16, 1901, p. 3
lxxxii St. Louis Republic, January 23, 1902, p. 1
lxxxii Ibid
lxxxii St. Louis Republic, January 24, 1902, p. 1
lxxxii St. Louis Post-Dispatch, October 25, 1902, p. 1
lxxxii St. Louis Post-Dispatch, December 15, 1903, p. 1
lxxxii St. Louis Post-Dispatch, May 21, 1904, p. 2

Chapter 8
lxxxii St. Louis Post Dispatch, April 28, 1902, p. 1
lxxxii St. Louis Post-Dispatch, January 11, 1904, p. 2

Chapter 9
lxxxii St. Louis Republic, October 30, 1904, p. 29
lxxxii Ibid
lxxxii St. Louis Post-Dispatch, October 25, 1904, p. 4

Chapter 10
lxxxii St. Louis Republic, January 7, 1903, p. 1
lxxxii St. Louis Post-Dispatch, March 13, 1897, p. 1
lxxxii St. Louis Post-Dispatch, January 7, 1903, p. 1
lxxxii Ibid
lxxxii St. Louis Republic, August 15, 1904, p. 1
lxxxii Ibid
lxxxii Shootout on Pine Street by author

Chapter 11
lxxxii St. Louis Post-Dispatch, January 25, 1903, p. 29
lxxxii St. Louis Post-Dispatch, February 2, 1903, p. 1
lxxxii St. Louis Post-Dispatch, June 26, 1903, p. 2
lxxxii Ibid

[lxxxii] St. Louis Post-Dispatch, June 28, 1903, p. 9
[lxxxii] Ibid
[lxxxii] Ibid
[lxxxii] St. Louis Post-Dispatch, July 5, 1903, p. 25
[lxxxii] Missouri Penitentiary Records
[lxxxii] St. Louis Star and Times, December 23, 1918, p. 15

Chapter 12
[lxxxii] St. Louis Post-Dispatch, January 26, 1907, p. 2

Conclusion
[lxxxii] St. Louis Post-Dispatch, July 4, 1916, p. 1

www.ingramcontent.com/pod-product-compliance
Lightning Source LLC
LaVergne TN
LVHW021236080526
838199LV00088B/4535